Your Eyes

WILL BE MY

Window

SERIES EDITOR

Nicole Walker

SERIES ADVISORY BOARD

Stephen Fellner

Kiese Laymon

Lia Purpura

Paisley Rekdal

Wendy S. Walters

Elissa Washuta

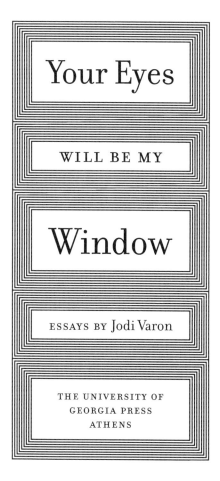

Your Eyes

WILL BE MY

Window

ESSAYS BY Jodi Varon

THE UNIVERSITY OF
GEORGIA PRESS
ATHENS

Published by the University of Georgia Press
Athens, Georgia 30602
www.ugapress.org
© 2023 by Jodi Varon
All rights reserved
Designed by Kaelin Chappell Broaddus
Set in 11/14 Garamond Premier Pro Regular
by Kaelin Chappell Broaddus
Printed and bound by Sheridan Books, Inc.
The paper in this book meets the guidelines for permanence
and durability of the Committee on Production Guidelines for
Book Longevity of the Council on Library Resources.

Most University of Georgia Press titles are
available from popular e-book vendors.

Printed in the United States of America
23 24 25 26 27 C 5 4 3 2 1

Library of Congress Cataloging-in-Publication Data
Names: Varon, Jodi, 1953– author.
Title: Your eyes will be my window : essays / Jodi Varon.
Description: Athens : The University of Georgia Press, [2023] |
Series: Crux: the Georgia series in literary nonfiction |
Includes bibliographical references.
Identifiers: LCCN 2023001497 (print) |
LCCN 2023001498 (ebook) | ISBN 9780820364667 (paperback) |
ISBN 9780820364674 (epub) | ISBN 9780820364681 (pdf)
Subjects: LCSH: Holocaust, Jewish (1939–1945)—Ukraine. |
Holocaust victims—Ukraine. | Holocaust memorials.
Classification: LCC DS135.U4 V28 2023 (print) | LCC DS135.U4 (ebook) |
DDC 940.53/1809477—dc23/eng/20230309
LC record available at https://lccn.loc.gov/2023001497
LC ebook record available at https://lccn.loc.gov/2023001498

I ate with delight my slice of happiness.

—ANNA ŚWIRSZCZYŃSKA

CONTENTS

PART FOUR
Your Eyes Will Be My Window

Your Eyes

WILL BE MY

Window

PROLOGUE

The Canadian poet A. M. Klein spent the first year of his childhood in Ratne, Ukraine, my grandmother's childhood home. In his poem "Dialogue," Klein imagines two bubbies speaking at a fishmonger's stall, and one old woman says she longs for Ratne's swamp, "even Ratno's muds." People in and outside the family joked that Poland was the swampy place where Jews lived, and this confused me, because Ratne, spelled Ratno then, was in the territory designated as the delimiting Russian Pale of Settlement when my grandmother was a girl there and also when her immediate family fled. If she held allegiance to the Russian Empire or the Second Polish Republic, Ukraine, or Israel, I did not know it; her allegiance as I perceived it was to her American family and to her efforts to bury the past. Inasmuch as she only lost one daughter, raised five children to adulthood, and survived both her husbands, she was successful. She transformed grief and longing for Esta Plat and others left behind in Ratne into sheets of honey cake, mountains of latkes, ziggurats of crewelwork doilies, peaches numinous as the jellyfish washed up on a pretty beach in Tel Aviv.

The past continued to evolve and grow with unbridled energy though, as the past is not governed by the same growth rates as the present. All but a handful of Jews and non-Jews were massacred in Ratne in 1942; my grandmother could not bury any of them.

I never heard my grandmother say the name of her village or her real maiden name, and it was two decades after her death that I began to hear and piece together what I believe are the fuller aspects of her life. These details of concealment and erasure are not remarkable for a person or a family coming to America to begin again after yet another generational displacement. Oddly, I thought, her Yiddish, as I began to repeat it as I grew older, was different than the Yiddish I heard in other Jewish circles, because her Yiddish was infused with Russian and Ukrainian rather than the more elegant tongues of countries that eventually annihilated their Jews, too.

A more accurate aspect of my grandmother's life in Denver, America, is that she did not escape the past, real or imagined. Many Denver neighborhoods were segregated, and the Ku Klux Klan was active and visible in Denver when my grandparents were trying to learn English and later when my mother and her siblings were small. The KKK burned crosses on Ruby Hill, not far from the Jewish community's center. Jews of my grandparents' class lived on the west side of Denver, in a close-knit community where the gas station my family patronized was owned by Izzie Segal, the drug store by Lou Tobin. A non-Jewish doctor never touched any of my family's bodies, and my grandmother shopped at Mildred's Kosher Grocery on the corner of Newton Street and West Colfax Avenue, famous for its thick slabs of marbled vanilla-chocolate halvah.

At the start of World War II, my grandmother's first husband, Harry, was dying of pancreatic cancer, and the letters she received from Esta Plat stopped arriving in 1942. The anxiety in my grandmother's house by the time I was born in the early 1950s felt like an ice fog, even in July. When I was young and came inside after picking red hollyhocks to make toothpick ballerinas with petal tutus, I thought her switch to Yiddish while conversing with her daughters was because she was discussing sex or us naughty grandchildren. In fact, she was trying to find the words to describe how to scale the wall of grief in front of her that reached to heaven, using just her fingernails.

The little girl I was knew we were deep in something, because my family, like so many others, had fled the other European something to land in America. I eventually learned Adorno survived until he didn't, that life for some continued after Auschwitz, but at what cost?

In spite of history, and also because of it, I was raised by parents who refused to be thought of as pitiful. My mother was a book-keeper and my father drove a taxi. They lived without thinking of themselves as victims. They did not hate life, or at least my father didn't. He had contributed to the war effort in the U.S. Army Air Corps, and the energy of that experience, good and bad, propelled him forward, always, without regret, for the remainder of his life. His laugh sounded like a phlegmy chuff and he liked to chuff at his own jokes. He loved to eat French pastry. He moved freely outside of the boundaries of Jewish west Denver and gambled with zeal until he lost all his money.

My mother, though, who as the youngest child and the family *mezinke*, the last daughter to marry and therefore the dutiful daughter who takes care of family members as they age, was the receptor of her mother's sorrow, grief, and guilt. For her, as for my grandmother, the past escalated until it surpassed the present. Masked, throttled, suppressed, it never disappeared. Worse became unbearable, until my grandmother escaped into dementia. My mother could not find a way to escape. Brutal, volatile, and violent as my young mother, when old she stopped taking care of her body and parked her butt in a wheelchair until her heart stopped working. I thought I could escape the death sentence of our past by living my life and raising a family in the rural Rocky Mountain West where few Jews live, but I surrounded myself in a kibbutz of the mind, in spirit and in fact, more comfortable with growing cucumbers than praying in a shul, eager to learn the secrets of cultivation denied my ancestors as stateless, landless Jews.

Before my grandmother's family was exiled and resettled in Ratne, administered by Russia / Poland / Germany / Soviet Union / Ukraine, they most likely lived in Germany. They bore a sense of shame for having lived and worked and wallowed in muck close to what is now Belarus's border with Ukraine on the edge of the Pripyat River's swamps. Instead of elegant, learned, and urbane ancestors from Odesa, Vilnius, Berlin, or Kraków, ancestors from the shtetlach in that part of the borderlands were associated with the ignorant dwellers of mythic Polish Chełm, mocked for their pious stupidity and meager, scrap-wood shanties, their odd, inflected Yiddish that some said sounded like braying goats. The stink of onions scented their breath, and donkey and goat shit piled up in their streets. The superstitions of their rebbes and their subjugation stretched like lightning from the sky to the root of every living thing permitted to live in the farthest wastelands of the empire.

People say that Judaism is the rhetoric of sky, and perhaps that is what sustained them. What a gorgeous phrase that is, rhetoric of sky, though only once in my adult life have I felt anything approaching that kind of spiritual generosity and grace. I never explored the etiology of faith with my grandmother; she taught me to recite the Shema before bed and introduced me to pink and turquoise blue Hostess Snoballs, which I assume had been okayed for consumption by the Union of Orthodox Rabbis, who regulated what grocery products she and other devout American Jews could eat.

I waited until everyone in my mother's generation had died before I could begin to address how the past had spiraled unbridled with the full force of catastrophe. I had done the same with my father and his family, but his story was more jubilant, sun-infused, bordering on joy, almost. His was an upbeat survivor's tale. Whoever was left behind in Thessaloniki, Edirne, or Andalusia, he did not wear a mantle of grief for them as his overcoat.

What is different now is that history makes new demands of everyone that are the same demands. On January 6, 2021, I was returning home from skiing on Lolo Pass outside Missoula and listened on the car radio to sounds of the insurrection at the Capitol unfolding in real time. I called my older son, Joshua, to see if he and his family were safe. They were. I realize I could have dialed another number where another mother's son would have pleaded desperately for help. When I returned home, I opened the file for this book, and the magnetic field of the Holocaust merged with our American flirtations with the same: the lies, the violence, the raw hatred, the dismantling of democracy in an unrepentant grab for power at any cost.

The ambiguous hope implied in the phrase "a rhetoric of sky" is compromised. There is no community, however insular, that is unaffected now. The same was true then, but as a child, I could only sense it when I saw my grandmother's hands covered with burns and bruises whose origins I couldn't fathom.

In 2005 a friend at the university where I teach helped to arrange a residency during my husband's and my first sabbatical year at the Ludwigsburg University of Education in Baden-Württemberg, not far from Stuttgart. I thought then, and continued to think for the next decade as my husband and I returned to Ludwigsburg to teach seminars in American life and culture, that living in proximity to other German cities and in a town whose size was easily navigable would enable me to understand how European communities bear and shape the act of remembering the legacy of shame for sacrificing others in the name of national solidarity and the hysterias of war.

In 2005, memorials to murdered Jews in Ludwigsburg and throughout Germany were scant, absent, works in progress, disputed, or in disrepair, and over the course of the next eleven years a renaissance to reshape death coincided with my private search to make over the endgame of the Holocaust.

My mother died on August 4, 2005, and while she was in hospice, I did not mention that I was going to teach in Germany, a country's name we were forbidden to say when I was growing up, let alone to visit. My husband and I arrived in Germany in September 2005, in time to say the Kaddish for my mother, for the first time, during Yom Kippur. This was important for me. I thought my mother would appreciate the gesture, the nod to ritual she had practiced throughout her life, but frankly, I'm not certain of this. More honest would be to say that when my mother died I was at a loss of how to move forward, fearful that I too would sink into the muck that consumed my grandmother and sank her into end days in dementia.

The gown and sheet covering my mother on the gurney in the mortuary were a shade of green I had never seen in nature, and I still recall how, that autumn and in many seasons after, green faded to gray as the skies darkened and the days grew short and drizzly. Eventually, greens intensified. They became defiant, pulsing, deeply verdant in the firs along the reforested slopes of the Schwarzwald and in all of the valleys of someone else's fatherland.

PART ONE

Songs for a
Blue Piano

War Artists

O NCE DURING WHAT TO ME IS THE MYSTIFYING free-for-all Germans call *Bahnschwimmen*, I looked along the deck of the pool on Berliner Platz in Ludwigsburg as I was taking a breath before another freestyle lap. A man in dark green swimming trunks walked along the deck from the back of the natatorium near the kiddie wading pool.

The man stepped gingerly on tiptoe like one traversing a bed of hot coals, along his shoulders and back a hideous scar from his neck to his waist, as though he had once crawled through burning timbers and had lost all the skin on his back. Grafts had healed with keloids along the edges of the wounds, and discolored, striated, lighter skin defined those borders. I swam the rest of that chaotic lap dodging the inevitable kicks to the gut and slaps in the face from swimmers doing the breaststroke poorly, my mind enveloped in the flames of burning buildings in Dresden, Düsseldorf, and Stuttgart, not the first time I had imagined such conflagrations. I imagined how the burned man on the pool deck might have crawled during the blaze with his face next to the floor searching for oxygen. I was reminded, too, of the oxygen tubes that slipped out of my mother's nose during her last days, and of the oxygenless wall I slammed against several years ago during a house fire, when I senselessly rushed toward the smoke with a wet hand towel, thinking I might be able to suppress the flames on a sheet of drywall that had ignited next to the furnace.

It was only the man's back that was burned. Not his legs, not his arms, not the thin, tight skin around his ankles or his long and bony feet. I could not see his face, though by his measured gait, his gray hair, his thinly muscled legs and thighs, I estimated his age to be about seventy. His disfigurement was grotesque and transfixing, and I thought him brave to parade around in public without his shirt.

As the man approached the lap pool, I swam past him again. He stepped gingerly on the pool deck like someone unaccustomed to going barefoot. My swim goggles had fogged up, so I stopped to wipe out the moisture on the lenses with my finger.

A beige beach towel decorated with oversized red roses draped across the man's shoulders and back. Perhaps he was seventy, but he had a full head of thick hair, worn longer than most men in Baden-Württemberg at the time. The man was narrow chested and narrow hipped, no beer, bread, and cheese belly like some of the other swimmers. When he draped the towel across one of the vacant chaise lounges at the deep end of the pool, his back was flushed red and smooth, unblemished, unscarred, his scapulae protruding like a trussed and roasted game bird's. He must have just exited the sauna. He plopped in one bony mass into the water. He wasn't buoyant and sank for a few seconds before he scissors kicked and his head popped up above the water's surface.

The man made his way across the pool little by little, hugging the wall. At the shallow end, the wall had a foot-wide tiled ledge several feet below the surface of the water. He stood up on the ledge and got out, his swimming trunks folding over in mismatched pleats that clung tightly to his thighs and buttocks, the water running off in sheets. He appeared to be enjoying himself, walking around in his trunks under a Plexiglas dome. He didn't wear his history on his skin; he wore a gaudy beach towel, a Kaufland special from one of their bargain bins near the supermarket entryway, where we often met our upstairs neighbor Mrs. K— buying Kalamata olives. I invented the man's scars, wincing, as the Latin poet Lucretius said, from grief's imaginary blows.

On the edge of Roßwag, a short train ride northwest of Ludwigsburg, my husband, David, and I took a Sunday stroll with friends along a footpath hugging the bank of the Enz River below the Wolf Cave cliffs. Lore says the besieged seventeenth-century citizens of Roßwag threw their dead off of those cliffs during the Thirty Years' War, unable to safely bury them. The acceleration of rot, stink, and concomitant disease accompanied by the growls and snarls from wolves devouring carrion seemed impossible to conjure in that mottled green-yellow linden shade, the river merrily burbling, our bellies full of sausage spiced with sage, sunflower-seed rolls with quince marmalade from our hosts' orchard fruit, cherries from the Turkish greengrocer's stand at the Saturday farmers market we'd brought along from Ludwigsburg. The rolling green and amber fields to our right thickened with oats and barley, air just shy of cloying. The colors reminded Heide, she said, of the hues favored by the wallpaper factory in nearby Rixheim, where Jacqueline Kennedy had purchased paper for the Oval Office of scenes from the American Revolution.

We have known our hosts, the Brudis, since the late 1980s, when Christoph, a German professor of art, was a visiting artist at our university, and Heide and her younger son were my students. Since then, we have tried to keep a cordial thread running through our relationship, on each return to Germany testing the sutures still remaining from the wreckage our countries wrought.

Two years after Christoph and Heide returned to Germany, their older son slipped on rain-slicked scaffolding and fell to his death at a construction site in Asia. Because our intimacy with them is tentative, we never spoke in detail about this tragic death. Once, walking through the small cemetery in their village on our way to their barn on the edge of Roßwag to retrieve four bicycles for all of us to ride, we approached their son's well-tended grave and watched bees harvesting the pollen on the tiny pink bell-shaped heather blossoms covering his plot. Reading his chiseled name on the headstone, I searched for words of condolence to say aloud but found none good enough. Each of us gave over to watching bees' transparent wings fluttering as they held their bodies aloft and plunged their heads inside the blossoms, working the heathers' stigmas for pollen grains, filling the pollen sacks on their legs until their legs seemed wrapped in bulging yellow mufflers, specks of pollen stuck to all their spindle hairs.

Hothouse peonies in her father's greenhouse surrounded Heide in early childhood, pinks, whites, deep maroons, but rather than the gaudy flowers' subtle scent given off as she rode among huge buckets filled with flowers while her father transported the peonies to market, the prevalent aroma lingering from her childhood is the slightly oily, rancid bite of unreconstituted powder from the meal packets distributed by the U.S. military authority in Stuttgart in the years immediately following World War II. Christoph too conjured that salty powder and its consistency of sand, but fumes from an unexploded incendiary bomb crowd his childhood reminiscences of scent. Fuel from the bomb leaked underneath the sill of his grandmother's door during one of the Allied bombings near Munich, where he waited in his grandmother's house for his father's return. His father was somewhere in the unidentified east, on duty. Fumes from the viscous liquid squeezed oxygen into corners of the house, magnesium and iron-infused fluid spreading silently across the carpet and the floor underneath it, the unexploded bomb leaking puddles of unignited fire.

My grandmother Susha's potato kugel warming in the pie safe in her oven lingers among my childhood's scents, baked grated potatoes, eggs, and corn oil folded into a batter thick as three stacked pancakes baked crisp. Food aromas merged with the islands of scent on her face discovered when my younger sister and I slept with her some weekend nights, the fine hairs around her lips slightly salty, her throat sweet with rose-infused toilet water, a metallic afterthought from the clips on her earrings rubbed off on her lobes.

A man dressed in dirty blue jeans and a white T-shirt walked toward us on the river path. In that part of Swabia, people aspired to meticulous cleanliness, especially on a Sunday. The man was lean and tall, young, I thought at first, his brown hair thick and short, face unshaven, the muscles in his arms elongated and hard from work instead of lifting gym weights, a tattoo of blurred and unspecified design the length of his right arm. Local factories like the ones in Bietigheim-Bissingen employed many workers from the former East Germany, Croatia, Kosovo, Romania, Slovakia. Perhaps he was one of those workers from a foreign place. He aged as he drew closer; what I'd assumed was shadow on his brow were age's furrows, veins in his arms barely visible from a distance now pronounced, the tattoo on his right arm a scar. The man quickly took our measure—four old Germans in ugly walking shoes acting like they owned the world.

As the man drew closer, Christoph's arm froze, outstretched. He cupped his hand, holding kernels of ripening barley separated from a sheaf he had picked along the edge of the path. He closed his fist over the kernels as he watched the man approach. Heide stepped to close the space between her and me across the path and threaded her arm in mine. David stepped forward next to Christoph, both of them in front of us.

Though I have worked for decades trying to dampen my fear of fantastical harm, Christoph's squared-back shoulders, his braced legs, and his clenched fist required at least a tempered gaze. By then we had formed a wall across the path in front of the man. I tried to see what Christoph saw: the man's lips—was that a sneer? A challenge? His unaccented silence—was he hiding an identity he knew would be revealed through speech? His presence on the path in Roßwag—were there recent incidents with workers we knew nothing about? A mugging? A stabbing? A slur? If none of these, was there a tacit understanding among the locals of who could walk where, and when? I wanted someone to tell me what to be afraid of.

The man leaned away from the path toward the high barley sheaves, the straight line of his lips moistened as he spat. The barley field glinted in the setting sun and rippled like a flag. Christoph greeted the stranger again, as an underling this time, claiming the formal hierarchy German grammar doles. Still, the man made no response. A rank odor like raw, putrefied liver and river mud wafted through the air. The man's eyes did not meet Christoph's eyes.

"*Grüß Gott*," Christoph said, again.

The man responded with a *shhh* sound pushed across his tongue and extruded through his teeth. We lined up one behind the other so that he could pass. The last of the day's sun before it set below a line of trees to the west briefly touched the mouth of the Wolf Cave, where Heide and Christoph's young sons had hidden one New Year's Eve in the hours before dawn, a thin wool blanket and a thermos of coffee between them as they smoked their father's pilfered cigarettes until nicotine made them dizzy.

Christoph's father, Walter Brudi, painted an abstract watercolor of a Russian washerwoman in 1942. The precise location of the village where the woman lived isn't identified, though Christoph said his father's wartime letters while he served as a *Kriegsmaler*, war artist, were posted from Russian villages now in eastern Ukraine. Deepened in sepia tones, the painting depicts a blocky woman, her head and neck covered with a babushka. She bends over a wash basin balanced atop a barrel, her sleeves pushed up to her elbows. Clothed as though to toil in the cold and mud, her thick torso is draped in gray, long black skirt brushing the tops of her mud boots. She bends in profile, her eye, nose, and upper lip outlined by her headscarf with its delicate pattern of roses, white patches suggesting illumination, a candle's beam or the moon shining on her head, back, the mound of washing, and the water buckets she used to fill her basin. The background is geometric blocks, swathes of black, smoke or night, and deep curves define her frame. Represented with brisk rather than detailed strokes, the woman's posture suggests that her task of cleaning a pile of laundry isn't done in haste.

My grandmother Susha too was from a Russian village, in the western province of Volyn, now in Ukraine. She owned a Westinghouse washer, vintage 1948, boasting a "fluid cushion of water" and fuses in the motor advertised "not to blow." The agitator in the barrel-like drum was vicious, the wringer mounted atop the barrel responsible for more than one fingertip-crushing by older cousins who liked to try to feed cousins' fingers smaller than theirs into the wringer. The machine was so loud and ambulatory my grandmother usually washed her clothes in the bathtub or on a washboard at the bottom of the summer kitchen steps next to the lilac bush in her backyard.

Susha's childhood playmate, Esta Plat, had likely grown as portly as the washer woman in the painting, during the forty years elapsed since she and my grandmother said goodbye to one another when their childhood ended. Esta Plat likely found resilience in the abundant yellows and greens of the sunflower fields for which Ukraine is noted. She likely ate the honey from the bees who worked that pollen. Unlike Susha, Esta Plat did not own a Westinghouse washing machine, though Ratne was electrified during the late 1920s, when the Second Polish Republic administered that territory of Ukraine. When Ukraine gained its independence from the former Soviet Union, Ratno became Ratne.

Unlike Susha, Esta Plat did not emigrate. This friend and cousin of my grandmother's survived two more pogroms and World War I. She married, went to Ratne's makeshift theater with her husband to see the same Yiddish version of *Hamlet* my grandmother and her husband likely saw in Denver, had a business, hired employees. Harvesters in her employ scoured the forest floor in the northern part of Volyn Province to search for wild mushrooms, which she dried and shipped to Warsaw, then on to customers in the United States, Argentina, Canada, and Palestine, where many of her Ratne countrymen now lived.

My grandmother was one of her customers, and she bought Esta Plat's mushrooms as a token from the Old Country, sent to her alongside Esta Plat's letters, which Susha saved just shy of sixty years, in a bundle tied with a frayed yellow ribbon. Not a voluminous number of letters lovingly preserved and archived like the war artist's letters, perhaps one or two letters a year, mailed before Rosh Hashanah and again before Purim, and not a lot of mushrooms, just enough to flavor a special bean casserole my mother loved called cholent that my grandmother served at the conclusion of the holy Days of Awe.

There is no chronicle penned by Esta Plat of the magnificence of the golden grains grown in the breadbasket of eastern Europe so many have tried to rob. There are no bragging rights for Esta Plat's braided Sabbath egg-washed challah, no scribbled recipe for her cholent, no record of whether the forest mushrooms she sold were boletes or chanterelles, no observation of whether she clapped her hands in time with klezmer bands or sang like a Yiddish nightingale. She wasn't a union steward or the president of Ratne's first savings and loan bank. She wasn't a teacher in Ratne's first secular school, and she didn't learn to drive a tractor or shingle a roof to prepare for the family's resettlement on a kibbutz near Jerusalem. Neither did she join her fellow Ratners in resettlement in Buenos Aires. She didn't learn the tango. She didn't sit to have her portrait drawn by a famous artist, and her name does not appear in the necrology list of Ratne's Yizkor book, its oral history remembrance book of the dead (*Ratno: Story of a Destroyed Jewish Community*).

While sorting through Susha's possessions in 1965 to move her from the house where she had raised her large family on the west side of Denver to a small apartment on Holly Street closer to her children, grandchildren, and great-grandchildren on the east side of Denver, I was responsible for sorting the sideboard that housed the family photographs and my mother's Latin primers. My aunts had long since appropriated the valuables in the glassed-in cases above the drawers, crystal candy dishes from Prague and a punch bowl rimmed in gold leaf, the photographs of beauties with lustrous eyes, my great-aunt Clara's scandalous portrait in an off-the-shoulders gown. The image of my dazed and smooth-faced teenaged grandparents on their wedding day graces a wall of a Denver kosher-style deli, and another capturing my great-grandfather bedecked in phylacteries, work clothes, and in his black rubber milking boots is framed and hanging in my cousins' living room. They were the only members of our family to return to visit Ratne, where their tour guide took them to a barn with a Star of David on a ripped piece of wood nailed to a rafter in the hayloft, "evidence" the guide said, that Jews had once lived there.

Imagine my surprise when I found a bundle of letters in the sideboard drawer, "in Jewish," as my mother said, that is, in Yiddish, written with the Hebrew alphabet. My grandmother had been whisked out of her house during its last emptying, distracted by cousins with a strawberry sundae at Dairy Queen, but even if she'd been present, her mind was already jumbled, memory fraying at the edges.

I hesitated, always wary of my mother's mercurial temper and the menace of her hands. Should I show her the letters, even though she'd made it clear throughout my childhood that she never wanted to discuss any facet of the Old Country, ever? Should I interrupt the argument she was having with her oldest sister in the kitchen? Should I put the letters in the stack I'd started of the few remaining family portraits and hide them until I could decipher them myself?

I balked, not my first crimp in unequivocal devotion, and not my last.

I walked into the kitchen holding the bundle. My mother was pressing a tissue against her right palm, having cut herself on the broken handle of my grandfather's shaving mug. The mug sat, blood-smeared, on the table on top of a page of the *Rocky Mountain News*. When she saw the yellow ribbon wrapped around the letters, her face went white then flushed with rage.

If I'd looked closer, I would have seen the way the envelopes had dried and wrinkled from all the tears Susha shed on them when my mother was a child. If I were clever, I'd have noticed the smudges of ink underneath Susha's fingernails no matter how often she scrubbed them. I would have smelled the heavy, waxy odor of her Revlon lipstick, the residue of time and gesture as she pressed her lips to the yellow ribbon that bound the letters. I could know these tangibles of grief, but I couldn't know, shouldn't know, what lost world those letters held.

As a way to liberate herself, finally and forever, my mother said, "Toss everything! We're throwing out all the useless dreck!"—the vials of my grandmother's hoarded rose-scented toilet water reverted to alcohol, the tangled flesh-tone support stockings with holes in the toes she never got around to darning, the costume jewelry with green and red glass jewels chipped or missing from a tiny caravan of dromedary camels and an elephant like ones Hannibal's army rode over the Alps to Rome.

The garbage barrel was nearly full. I tossed the letters on top of the gallon jars of honey we found in Susha's cellar near the boarded-over coal chute, jars filled with so many ants the honey looked like amber.

When I was still a child, I threw away Esta Plat's letters to my grandmother, the only detailed record of Esta's life. What could a bundle of letters, and from the Old Country, contain? What might they mean to our diminished family, shocked and stunned into silence in a time warp that tried every day to erase each year before 1945?

What if at least Esta Plat's letters had survived, like other families' heirlooms?

I didn't even think to save the pretty stamps.

Songs for a
Blue Piano

A COMPACT, WIRY MAN IN A SHORT-SLEEVED BLUE shirt and khaki pants sprawled on his second-story window ledge above the Synagogenplatz, Ludwigsburg's Synagogue Square memorial. Smoke rings floated away from his face, drifted, thinning until they looked like dryer lint suspended in the air. He flicked the burning stub of his cigarette down to the gravel, where it joined wadded fliers from a home-delivery pizza vendor, beer cans, and a soiled diaper whose tabs had come undone.

Around the periphery of Ludwigsburg's vanished synagogue, paving stones in the gravel marked the outline of the synagogue that was. Indents noted where the synagogue's heavy, timber doors once stood and where the Ark of the Covenant lodged the congregation's Torah until the two-day countrywide pogrom of Kristallnacht on November 9–10, 1938, compelled Ludwigsburg's patriotic fascist fathers to incinerate it along with all the other synagogues in Germany. The charred, unstable husk of the synagogue's skeleton was exploded a few days later, after the foundation stones were removed and repurposed to reinforce Ludwigsburg's prison walls.

From 1938 until 1988, when the first memorial at the synagogue site was designed, the empty square was a children's playground.

On the northeast corner of the synagogue's outline, a small, rectangular bronze plaque was etched with the synagogue's image, a Byzantine-styled, compact two-story building with a cupola dome over the main door. The synagogue was erected in 1884, and by 1900, 234 citizens of Ludwigsburg prayed there; in 1934 the congregation celebrated the synagogue's fiftieth anniversary.

Ten scrawny linden trees planted inside the perimeter of what was once the synagogue's interior stood in three short zigzag rows with a single tree at the head, to depict the Tree of the *Sefirot*, a visual schematic of the imagination of God, according to the Kabbalah. From the vantage of the man blowing smoke rings from his window ledge, the trees formed a rough hexagon with shriveled leaves on the tips of scrawny stems, a rotting grove stunted in gravel and standing water. The huge granite memorial stone at the western edge of the square attempted somber dignity, and the pebbles lined along its base and at its top signified Jewish visitors' presence at the site marking the ashes of one of God's incinerated houses framed by the rhetoric of sky.

Each time David and I went to the plaza under an impenetrable blanket of clouds before Shabbat or on our way to Stuttgart, we stood alone, though on each visit more and more pebbles lined the base of the granite memorial stone, along with purple mums and potted heather plants placed at the base of a manicured privet hedge. Later that autumn, there was a candle-lighting ceremony on the anniversary of Kristallnacht, but we learned of it only by walking through the plaza afterward, where melted candle wax and stones painted white with the names of detained and deported Ludwigsburger Jews were lined along the memorial's granite base. The sense of looming human presence was palpable in the square, as everywhere in Europe, which made going there enticing, disappointing, and fraught, always half-expecting revelation, snipers, an impending putsch, or the punch of loss.

A blow in the chest is how early visits to the Synagogenplatz felt, amplified by the memorial's squalid gray palette and its stink of fetid water. Each scuff along the gravel path evoked the shattering of glass, the odors of men's hysteria—armpit stink, overheated semen in the crotches of their heavy blue serge trousers, the arousal from their purifying flames fanned by thoughts of righteous violence against the *Ungeziefer* vermin among them.

On a train to Stuttgart to worship on Yom Kippur in the rebuilt and functioning Neue Synagoge, David and I gazed out the train window trying to see what we can never see—his young, dead father, my old, dead mother suddenly alive again, only to have now to worry, wondering if I'd lost my mind. I saw her as she was before her last illness, dressed in her favorite pink and green-flowered muumuu, sitting at her kitchen table shuffling a deck of cards, watching a Colorado Rockies baseball game. She shuffles one more time before dealing herself another hand of solitaire in a heaven she never imagined.

The depraved worlds of the vanished are now this world, with its kiosks selling honey-scented beeswax candles shaped like pine cones and with its vanilla-flavored crepes at a stand near the Schwabstraße line's exit into central Stuttgart. Orchids line interior sills, landscaped yards and privet hedges blurred to a green smudge as the train approaches Stuttgart.

We were told by synagogue staff that a buzz would signal the unlocking of the metal security door, beyond it a shell of reinforced concrete encasing and protecting the Neue Synagoge from arson and bomb attempts. The surveillance camera above the door, we learned, would swivel to train its lens on us. Nothing to be alarmed about at all.

While we waited, the camera turned and pointed down the

street, where two bicyclists carried a ten-foot ladder between them. Each rider held onto a different rung, one partway down the ladder, the other a little farther, just enough for the two of them to distribute the weight of the ladder while remaining upright on their bicycles. The woman sat erect on her bicycle saddle, determination playing across her knitted brow. She balanced with care, her shirtsleeves rolled to the elbow on that balmy morning. The man seemed less confident, syncopating his pedaling behind his partner, gripping one handlebar, the fingers of his other hand awkwardly splayed along the ladder's rung. Sunlight refracted crannies in the rungs as silver rays, and as the bicyclists came closer, the camera adjusted its cant to focus on the area between the door and the odd beast riding past. The bicyclists noted our presence without turning their heads, without breaking their rhythm, or speaking, the only sound their breathing and their tires rolling over asphalt. As they pedaled on, away from the periphery of the synagogue's security zone, the camera lingered on their movement, hesitated, swiveled, watched until they slowly disappeared down the street and the glint of silver from the ladder's reflection annealed to the last drops of dew on the sidewalk. It surveilled the space between freedom to worship and danger's sphere, watching for random movement and trying to access real from imagined harm.

As soon as our passports were collected, we moved to the foyer in front of the main sanctuary, where a memorial for congregants who had fought in World War I was prominently displayed alongside the charred remains of some of the books from the synagogue's library snatched from burning embers during Kristallnacht. As we read the long list of surnames, an usher approached us, directing David to the main floor of the sanctuary and me to the balcony's segregated women's seating.

At first, I was alone on the women's balcony. The crests from the Twelve Tribes of Israel were fastened on banners near the ceiling, and above the altar, a clearstory of yellow and orange stained glass filtered sunlight into flaxen strands. Rows of high-backed wooden seats stretched down steep stairs to the balcony rail, brass name-plates fastened to the high backrests.

Soon enough, footsteps announced another congregant, and I held my breath wondering if it was her seat I was occupying. A short, broad, and buxom woman covered head to toe in white stood at the top of the stairs. As she started down, her tight-fitting mid-calf-length sheath rustled, the buttons on her rayon blouse straining across the fullest part of her breasts. A crocheted shawl was draped across her shoulders. As she descended, she paused and tucked a few stray, copper-colored hairs back underneath her gauze head-scarf. All skin but her hands, wrists, face, lower part of her calves, and ankles were covered. Her left leg was fortified by a black elastic brace on her knee as she limped down the half-flight of pitched stairs. She clutched each aisle-seat backrest as she stepped down, her white canvas slip-ons squeaking like an unlubricated door.

Her gaze tallied my shoes, clothing, and jewelry, my watch, body tone, cosmetics, hair. Her thick-fingered, red-knuckled hands were adorned with rings—wedding band, amber pinkie ring, a pearl. She slipped on a pair of glasses, which magnified her thick mascara. "No, no, sit," she said, her lips pursed in a mock wince. She pressed her free hand palm down, tamping down thin air as I stood to give up my seat.

Though she had a choice of seats throughout the balcony, Galena P— sat beside me, in the seat whose nameplate identified the seat as Lilli M—'s. Perhaps it would have seemed rude to sit in the empty chamber so far removed from the only other guest, though I probably would have done just that. She scooched her buttocks around in the uncomfortable seat and opened the carved walnut lid of the compartment in front of her, took out a scented white hand-kerchief and unfolded it, tracing the delicate blue stitches of the embroidered *L*. She looked at me and smiled, held the handkerchief to her nose, inhaled the fragrance, wadded it up, and tossed it back inside. She likewise sniffed the opened roll of soft-shelled peppermint candies and the tip of the perfume atomizer after shaking the contents of the bottle and squirting mist on both her wrists. She gave her lips a fresh coat of red lipstick from its elegant Chanel black-and-gold cylinder then tossed it, too, back into the compartment.

"Numbers, there," she said, tilting her head, after our perfunctory introductions and her ten-second summary of Russian history that concluded with "Putin" followed by a mime of spitting. She pointed to a set of placards on the left-hand side of the bimah denoting the cantor's page and paragraph in the Russian version of the prayer book. "See?"

Her husband, in contrast to Galena's white, wore a suit of gangster-colored gold. He had taken his place on the bimah to turn the placards. He looked up at her, pushed his heavy, black-rimmed glasses up the bridge of his nose, ran a finger along the number placard hinges, and flipped placards back and forth to make sure they were functioning without squeaking. "At home, a rabbi, almost," she said. "But here, nothing. A studio apartment," she said, flicking her right hand. "Only Germans are good enough for Germans."

She leaned over the balcony railing to watch men trickle into the main floor of the sanctuary. I pointed to my husband. "Tall," she said, and nodded. "Very nice."

"At the end, the Germans will come. To say Kaddish, hear the shofar, and break the fast with apples dipped in honey and the food my cousin cooks." She bunched the fingertips on her right hand and pressed them to her lips in praise of his cuisine.

The din amplified as the synagogue filled. Men tall or stooped moved with elegant, determined steps, floated, almost, their black shoes polished and gleaming, their faces open, less guarded than their compatriots on the quiet morning streets of Stuttgart. They shook hands with gusto, clasping palms, registering the warmth of life. The shammash tried to silence the noisy chatter, but on both floors, congregants ignored him. When he pointed to the balcony, a stately woman stood and pointed the spine of her holiday siddur at him as she shook her head in defiance, and the shammash seemed to cower. A Black man strode down the aisle past the shammash, his white gauze caftan billowing as he moved. His children were enveloped in the cloud of his commanding stride, then took their seats in the front row while he shook hands with all the men around him. A *Zweimetermann*, a good head taller than all the rest, his yarmulke floating on thick waves of silver-and-white hair, followed behind. He took the aisle seat, spreading his tallit around his arms and back as though an eagle about to soar into the sky.

Galena's son-in-law and grandsons were seated near the back. She waved to them as they settled into their seats, then she motioned behind her to the last row of seats in the women's balcony to her daughter and granddaughters, who declined her silent invitation to move closer. They sat, instead, next to a woman with a square of white lace pinned to her hair, sitting with her daughters. "From Holland. The misses. With the Black man," Galena said, pointing to the sanctuary floor. "From Ethiopia."

"*Cha-ta-nu*!" ("We have sinned!") A man's shaken voice cracked as he shouted, disrupting the quiet during the silent Amidah prayers as congregants tapped their chests with their fists in a gesture of penance. "We have sinned. We have sinned. We have all sinned."

Women raised their heads from the pages of their prayer books and looked one to the other. Galena shook her head. As she puckered, her lipstick seeped into wrinkled channels between her nose and upper lip. No one seemed surprised by the man's outburst, but many seemed agitated, rubbed the backs of their hands, pressed their fingertips in the top buttonholes of their jacket lapels, tried to catch another's glance. The woman who had stared down the shammash before the service began peering over the balcony railing, gesturing to her husband sitting next to the man in the caftan. Her husband gathered up the edges of his tallit and started up the aisle to quiet the agitated man.

"*Cha-ta-nu!*" The man stood now in the aisle in the center of the sanctuary, visible to all but the women sitting in the highest rows of the balcony. His yarmulke was clipped to his thin, disheveled gray hair, and rather than a carefully chosen, immaculate, and well-pressed suit, he was dressed like a groundskeeper in gray slacks and a blue shirt. His tallit had slipped from his shoulders and sagged in a *U* at the middle of his back, held just above the floor by his bent elbows. He clutched a green apple studded with needles in one hand and moved it close to his lips, moaning as the needles began to prick him. Several men left their seats and came up behind him from the back, lifted his tallit onto his shoulders before it touched the ground. He swung slowly around and brandished the apple like a mace.

"This year, enough," the man who had moved from the front commanded in a booming voice.

"Executioners!" the man cried, an octave higher than his last outburst, and pressed the needles to his lips, harder, breaking his skin. Blood beaded on his lips and smeared the edge of his tallit as his hand began to shake. One man from behind clasped the penitent's wrist and squeezed until his apple mace fell to the ground.

After a brief skuffle, the apple was quickly wrapped in a handkerchief and removed from the sanctuary. The penitent moaned and his tallit fell to the ground. A few women gasped. Another man stood to pick up the tallit and the penitent's foot lashed out at the man's face still bent low to the ground. The man's nose spurted blood and his angry, whispered words filled the hall. The penitent went limp as two others threaded their arms underneath his armpits and moved him toward the exit to the foyer.

"Monsters! Traitors!" As he was sequestered outside the sanctuary, the penitent accused everyone in the congregation for masking their grief while he did not, clawing off their scabs of grief.

Galena nudged my arm. "Vodka," she whispered, shaking her head then tapping one finger on her temple as she winked, trying to dismiss the penitent's actions.

The sun beamed through the clearstory as though to mock the scene. Women standing to my left were bathed in light striated like mineral soil, pretending not to be afraid of the penitent's raw emotions, their lips relaxed to almost pleasant smiles belying their discomfort. One woman balanced her siddur on her armrest as she retied the scarf around her hair, while another smoothed the waves along her uncovered crown. As she swept her palm back from her temple, her blouse lifted from her skirt's waistband, exposing a tiny patch of skin.

As each congregant finished reading, she marked her place in the siddur and performed the last ritual of the Amidah, three steps back followed by three bows: left, right, forward. The women minced their dance steps in place in the narrow rows, while down below several of the men with aisle seats stepped into aisles to back up, bow, bend double, rise, and turn their faces toward the ark. I have always loved this dance, this devotion, release, renewal, but then, as now, perform it with self-conscious reserve and the knowledge of the many ways caps on grief explode.

As the cantor began to sing again, the balcony door opened. A chauffeur held firmly to a late arrival's arm at the top of the balcony stairs. Lilli M— squared her shoulders and tugged lightly at the edge of her emerald brocade suit jacket as she peered down the steps, slowly rotating the bracelet on her right wrist. She acknowledged Galena sitting in her seat, and with the assistance of her cane brought the full weight of her legs onto each step with the help of a long relay of women's hands and shoulders used as braces as she negotiated her descent. She stopped at the end of the row where Galena and I sat, expecting Galena to rise. Galena didn't rise.

I stood, apologetic. Galena looked straight ahead and squeezed the swollen, rounded curves of her knees underneath her skirt, snapped the elastic rim of her knee brace. Lilli cleared her throat and Galena caressed the armrests of Lilli M—'s seat, pretending not to hear. Lilli sighed theatrically.

"*Die Dame*," Galena muttered under her breath, "the lady." The woman on my left lightly tapped my arm, and in unison, every woman seated in our row moved one seat down, forcing Galena to give up Lilli's seat only when Lilli began to lower her frail haunch into Galena's lap.

Lilli smoothed her precision-tailored skirt, ran her delicate hand down the placket of her brocade jacket, and opened the lid of the compartment in front of her. She smoothed out the wrinkles in her wadded handkerchief and folded it into a tight square before she placed it back inside. She removed the top and twisted the tube of lipstick, noted the squashed tip, breathed in the scent of her perfume on Galena's skin. She proceeded to greet all of those around her, formally, lavishly, cheerfully, excluding Galena. She lightly took my hand as she moved her arm across Galena's torso. She switched to English, which Galena could not speak.

With practiced economy, Lilli said she had been sent away to English boarding school before the war, lost her family, had no children, tried to live with her second husband in Milwaukie, Miami, and Israel, then moved back to Stuttgart. "Unacceptable!" was how she concluded her recitation, cursing all the Russian Jews who had invaded her synagogue as she slapped the leg she called a "limp and useless piece of flesh."

The cantor continued, during the Kedushah added a litany of the death camp names throughout Europe during World War II, each name broken into syllables and sung. The singular, melodic names of all the dead—Bluma, Rukhele, Malka—became Majdanek instead, became Bełżec, Sobibór, Treblinka. On this holiest of days, the names wove their way into the fabric of the service, naming what is evil what is human what is anathema to mercy. The faces of every woman on the balcony pixilated, our hair and nails and tears. Our uteruses pixilated, the clusters of eggs in ovaries that belonged to the ovaries of our grandmothers, to their mothers, and theirs, to every unnamed Esta Plat. The cantor struck his chest with a closed fist after drenching every syllable in song. He swayed and bowed, winding his tallit tighter and tighter around himself until he looked like a white cocoon.

The death recitation concluded with the chanting of the Kaddish, my reason for attending. As all the congregants with living parents filed out of the sanctuary and the balcony and into the foyer, the ones with no living parents remained inside. I glanced at Lilli. She sat, fidgeting with her bracelet. Galena likewise sat, dabbed at her nose with a tissue she retrieved from between her breasts. The three of us withdrew into our private miseries. I was afraid not of what I might feel, but that I might feel nothing, might feel sealed off from love or duty or even sorrow, might feel shame or guilt for some as yet unimagined disregard or slight of the newly dead person my mother had become. I had tried unsuccessfully to seal up my grief. The cantor gestured for all to rise. We rose. The Kaddish did not comfort, but the melody did.

Why do some rush into the jaws of harm while others drag their feet? My mother was shunned by her own Ashkenazi Jewish community for having married an atheist Sephardi, then shunned again for divorcing him. She detested public outcries, demonstrations of faith, anything reeking of formalized religion, yet she too went to synagogue on Yom Kippur, in a renegade congregation that met in a repurposed Quonset hut not far from Susha's apartment on Holly Street. Though she said she went there for convenience's sake and because they didn't shun nonmembers, very few people knew her there and she relished the anonymity after decades of gossip about her role as Susha's fallen daughter. She could sit in the back in her wheelchair, and she didn't have to make excuses about not being able to fasten buttons or zippers or wrangle into pantyhose.

Once sharp and smartly dressed, and with hats and veils to match, on her very last Yom Kippur service, my mother sat in her wheelchair in her favorite rose-print muumuu and canvas slip-ons, picking at a thick scab on her hand. Lost in her own thoughts and unmoored in time, she hummed as the visiting cantor mumbled through selected portions of the service. As he was wrapping up and praising God, she and a handful of other Jewish residents at her assisted care facility watched with anticipation as an aide set out platters piled high with minichallahs then set up the boards for the bingo game to follow.

Back in our Ludwigsburg apartment courtyard, Ahmed, the fifth-grade boy whose family lived above us on Lortzingstraße, was playing with his little sister. She stood very still near our communal clothesline, her eyes squeezed tight, shoulders, back, and spine straight against a maple tree. The skirt of her dress was soiled with grass stains, and she held her hands clasped in front to cover the long green smear. Her small chin jutted forward, her neck arched like a swan's. A green apple balanced on her head as her brother aimed a rubber-tipped arrow from his drawn bowstring at the fruit on top of her head. We knew this young William Tell, because his mother had dragged him to our apartment door by his wrists to offer us his employ as a German tutor, though the family spoke only Turkish at home.

A slight breeze began to blow, and the sweet, heavy fragrance of the hydrangeas still in blossom in the courtyard mingled with smells of potatoes, stewing brussels sprouts, and a turkey roasting in someone's oven. Across the courtyard, a woman who could have been Galena's double sat in a blue chenille bathrobe on her second-floor balcony in front of an easel, alternately lifting a paintbrush and a cigarette, glancing into the courtyard then into the dark of her apartment, where someone was practicing piano.

The autumn wind unloosed some brittle leaves, and they drifted down in front of the little girl standing still as her brother's target. The leaves tickled her nose, and she reached her hand up to scratch. The apple fell off her head. Ahmed relaxed the tension on his bowstring, raised his arms, and scolded his sister, his bow in one hand, the arrow in the other. She rubbed a scab on her elbow and turned to watch a motorcycle buzz by in the street. Ahmed put his bow down on the grass. He walked over and picked up the apple, ran his thumb over the untouched green skin. His mother leaned out the second-story window overlooking the courtyard and called to them. He looked up without answering and took two big bites of the apple. He wiped his mouth on his sleeve and handed the apple to his sister, who finished eating it, core and all. He gave her the arrow to carry, then picked up the bow, grabbed her free hand, and led her inside.

Sad Angel

A TALE RECOUNTED BY RUSSIAN FOLKLORIST AND ethnographer S. Ansky (Solomon Rappoport, 1863–1920) explains how a person is constructed from a "drop" and built, drop by drop, by God. The first drop is sexed then bestowed with beauty or ugliness, intelligence or stupidity, experience or naivete, wealth or poverty, and if the drop, a fetus by now, doesn't like the gift package, too bad, because we all know God turns a deaf ear on protestations. Bright Angel plies the fetus with vivid memories of apples and apricots, peaches, figs, the taste of honey, the quadratic equation and Newtonian differentials, blows the scent of frangipani across its nostrils. Lips partly closed, Bright Angel hums in the fetus's ears all the unutterable names of God and the music of the spheres, explains the racing strategy in a peloton, rubs velvet on the fetus's forming arms, followed by a feather brushed lightly over genitals. Bright Angel promises to swaddle the newborn in flannel, silk, and gossamer.

Right before a birth, Sad Angel flaps its scraggly wings and hovers over the fetus's brow, blows the halitosis of forgetfulness into the fetus's breath, pushing away the lingering taste of *cronson* with their crushed walnut filling. The taste of dates and honey disappears, rosewater, the scent of turmeric and cloves, the sweet, gentle percussion of chimes, the sound of mother's lullabies. All is carried far away on the wind of forgetfulness. The child is born with only an ungraspable but no less vivid memory of having looked under the edge of the curtain of eternity, all knowledge now lost, memory accruing at great cost and sacrifice over a lifetime of study, devotion, experience, and single-minded absurdist pursuits.

I retold this folktale to my husband, and he said I didn't remember death's finale, before the soul is greeted by the angels' congress, ushered by Bright and Sad Angels holding hands. Sad Angel triumphs again, he said, and everything the soul had learned in life is lost, forgotten.

In my version, Bright Angel triumphs, and not only that, it presents the soul with a black velvet bag tied with a golden cord, inside beeswax and royal jelly, rosin dust, manna, rain collected on hot pavement in Jerusalem. There is also a vial of clove oil to soften beards and angels' coverts. The pouch is gifted like a necklace worn close to the face, or what was the face, like the scented hankies dipped in Jean Naté that bubbies carried to the synagogue on Yom Kippur to mitigate the armpit odors unleashed by penitents on hot autumn afternoons.

In Krzysztof Kieślowski's *The Double Life of Véronique*, two young women, doppelgängers, live one in Kraków during the breakup of the Eastern Bloc, the other in Paris. The Pole, Weronika, is a musician, a vocalist, and during her operatic debut, suffers a heart attack and dies on stage. Prior to her debut and death, Véronique, her Parisian doppelgänger, glimpses the Polish vocalist in Kraków at the edge of a student demonstration in Rynek Główny. Véronique, on a sight-seeing tour, is hurried onto the tour bus as the demonstrators surge. Weronika stands in the plaza at the edge of the crowd, after collecting sheet music knocked from her hands by a demonstrator and scattered by the wind. Without thinking or observing closely, Véronique photographs the woman, end of scene.

An artist/puppeteer performs a skit at the school where Véronique is a music teacher who favors chimes, and the skit's moribund conclusion is the resurrection of a young, small-waisted woman-puppet who dies suddenly, inexplicably, like Weronika. The butterfly wings representing the puppet's resurrection haunt Véronique, as she is haunted by Alexandre Fabbri, the handsome, charismatic puppeteer, read: God the puppet-master. Alexandre barrages her with phone calls backgrounded with white noise during which he does not speak. He sends a letter with a brown shoestring in it, an odd clue, which leads Véronique, via the letter's postmark from Gare Saint-Lazare, to the train station, symbolism loud, where she meets her stalker.

Infused with Véronique's beauty and his own sublime fantasies, Alexandre admits to performing a psychological experiment on Véronique, in order, of course, to write a book. Unsettled by Alexandre's stalking, Véronique flees the meeting; he pursues. During an intimate afternoon when they walk around a hotel room in their underpants, Véronique empties her purse onto the bed to better let her lover know her. Alexandre takes a close look at the wrinkled contact sheet of Véronique's Kraków sight-seeing tour. He points to her portrait, really Weronika in an oversized wool coat Véronique has never owned. At first Véronique seems offended that her lover would think she could own such an ugly coat, but on second glance, her face and Weronika's face are interchangeable. Véronique, overwhelmed by a nagging connection she has felt throughout her life to an unidentifiable other, is overcome with inexplicable grief. She does not know Weronika is dead, but then, she didn't know Weronika was alive, only that she had an ungraspable sense that she was always incomplete. And the handsome puppeteer? The trajectory of their love seems sullied by the puppeteer's manipulations and the death of Weronika, the double whom Véronique will never know but will always sense the absence of. As the film ends, Alexandre is in his workroom creating two puppet doubles for his next performance: Véronique and Weronika.

In proximity to a remembrance by Ben-Zion Kamintzky in the unabridged Yiddish version of the Ratne Yizkor book, there is a winter photograph of young couples standing on the wooden planks that were common pathways through the bogs surrounding Ratne. It looks like the mud is frozen underneath the planks. The trees are bare. The women wear knee-length, heavy winter coats, as do the men. The men also wear fedoras, an emblem of Mendel Blat's flourishing hat-making business in Ratne. From the cut of their coats and the couples' casual, modern air, it's probably the early to mid-1930s. None of the subjects in the photograph are named, but they look happy, or at least unconcerned, or maybe vaguely ignorant, or maybe just young, though not as young and nowhere as beautiful as Weronika. Their smiles are like my grandmother's as she posed in front of the family sedan a summer afternoon in 1942, in the mink stole my grandfather bought her after consolidating his earnings from being a policeman and distilling bathtub gin.

My grandmother's favorite Yiddish phrase, according to my mother, "We plan, God laughs," was bandied in our house as soon as my grandmother burned her forearm in the flame of her gas range, the first sign of her dementia. My mother wore the phrase like Bright Angel's empty pouch with all the manna scattered. She recited the phrase before she threw her body on top of my grandmother's casket at the gravesite before my grandmother's interment, and when my older sister tried to pack her suitcase and run away. When my father ran away, my mother visited the phrase when he returned. Every time I pleaded with her to let me join my friends on a road trip to the tip of South America, I learned that when we plan, God laughs.

When we plan, God laughs, but what does God's laugh sound like? C major, B minor, the Mixolydian mode? Does it sound like a three month old's glee when he hears his mother speaking for the stuffed armadillo in her hand, or is the laugh the sardonic chortle of a jaded politician? A dolphin's whistle? A ha ha or a hee-hee?

Not far from the town of Ratne, there is a conglomeration of hillocks called the Prokhid Hills. On the 13th of Elul, 5702 (August 26, 1942), the remaining Jews of Ratne met Sad Angel in the final *Aktion* against them. Absent were the fourteen agile men who had used the smoke caused by the incineration of Jewish people's houses as an opportunity to conceal themselves as they fled to the forest scraggly as Sad Angel's wings. Absent were those others who had emigrated at the turn of the twentieth century like my grandmother Susha and her family, to Denver, others to Toronto, Montreal, Buenos Aires, and Jerusalem. The fedora maker turned Judenrat commander, Mendel Blat, and between 1,300 and 1,500 other Jews were marched to a pit dug by Ukrainian farmers and slaughtered along with everyone else in the village by Ukrainian nationals and a German brigade of *Einsatzgruppen* commandos who had been rampaging in nearby towns.

One of the farmers who had helped to dig the pit, Ben-Zion Kamintzky recounted, survived and returned to the site that night, after the sound of gunfire finally stopped, but before all the pooled-up blood had seeped into the dirt, looking for Jew-gold and Jew-silver, Jew-jewelry, clothing, shoes, Bright Angel's black velvet pouch, anything he could cart away and sell someday. He said the untamped dirt that filled the pit heaved, surged, and buckled as the undead clawed their way up, or what they imagined to be up, like avalanche victims trying to guess where the air will be after somersaulting down a hill with snow and ripped-up trees on top of them. The farmer's tongue shriveled as he puked the undulations of clay and sand that clogged his throat, his nose incapable of breathing so much terror-laden air, his eyes covered with cataracts like an old man's eyes. His knuckles burst, nails folded under like yellow fungal toenails, and his hands turned to dust as his bowels heaved in concert with the mound. But rather than clawing at the mound or using the shovel he'd brought along to worry the dirt away from the partly buried rubies he was certain he would find, he stood there, paralyzed, doing nothing except watching until the undulations ceased. Kaput. Then, he ran away.

In the ensuing weeks and years when Stalin's troops raged all over Ukraine, everywhere the farmer listened he heard a sound he could almost recognize, the moaning of children calling out to him with thick cloth gags across their mouths. After that night in 1942, he pledged to God to help the Jews who remained in Ratne, though Ratne had no Jews. According to my husband's version of the Yiddish folktale, Sad Angel visited the farmer right before his death, obliterating guilt, his potential guilt, his memory of guilt, his progeny's inherited guilt, and the farmer spends eternity restringing all the angels' harps in heaven.

An equal opportunity destroyer, Sad Angel is, as far as dementia goes; it cannot wait for death. The farmer who had searched the dirt for Jew-jewels smelled Sad Angel breath waft across his nostrils, but he couldn't remember that prebirth stink and thought it was just the fecal smell of burst intestines. Old age marbled his eyes and Satan hid his pitchfork, Sad Angel erasing the farmer's path out of his field, hiding his smoker that cleared the bees out of his hives' supers so the farmer could harvest honey. How does one protect one's face from a million stings of bees? He couldn't recall. Where was the jolly, gold-toothed Jew he greeted in the market before the war? Which war? What's a Jew? The farmer couldn't count to ten.

If my grandmother's longing for her Ratne childhood friend Esta Plat were personified in wood, her puppet would be clothed in a brown wool, smartly tailored coat, red bumps like a necklace to approximate the allergic hives wool raised in a ring around my grandmother's neck. For my grandmother, Sad Angel was a repeat offender, returning not just at death, but fifteen years after her birth, when she emigrated. While she was bent double vomiting in steerage, Sad Angel blew the sardine onion breath of almost forgetting home across her face, and again, when she could no longer remember the sound of her first husband's voice, and again, when she forgot how to see with depth and so distinguish between a real person and a two-dimensional image on TV, and again, when she lost her mind completely. She became Sad Angel's punching bag. The crumbs of her remembering, like Véronique's photograph of a woman in a winter greatcoat in Kraków's Rynek Główny, tormented her. It wasn't only Esta Plat my grandmother forgot, it was everyone and every language she had learned. She croaked an unrecognizable garble of Polish, Yiddish, English, Russian, Ukrainian, and Hebrew, forgot the syntax of the Shema. She forgot how to close her eyes and fall asleep or form whole words with her lips and tongue and throat. She forgot how to breathe.

Dear Susha, Esta Plat might have written in a letter to my grandmother,

I've never seen the blue lark buntings you described. But, you remember tits and partridges, hedgehogs and blackcocks. We have hobos now, who lose their way on the path to the old city where the synagogue was torched; I don't know what happens to them, but I imagine they are shot. There is no roundhouse here or a rail line as you describe, but even if there were, the guards would make sure the hobos didn't ride for free. We call them vagabonds, włóczędzy; gentiles call them Jews. Russians call them Poles. Poles call them Ukrainians. We are done sending zlotys to the Great Yeshiva in Wilno [Vilnius] because it does no good. We have stopped believing in God. My man says we will go to Palestine like the others, but what use will an old woman be in the desert

sun? I don't know how to drive a tractor or hammer nails; I know how
to tend the bees and harvest forest mushrooms. There is no forest in the
desert. When Palestine was Canaan there was honey, but the cedars of
Lebanon were cut down long ago, if they ever stood. Maybe I will knit
some more. Thank you for the yarn.

Esta's surname, Plat, sounds like *blatt*, the name for a folio of the
Gemara, paper, and also the botanical leaf. Historically, common
people like Esta's family didn't merit surnames. Once the edict arrived from the tsar in 1844 to begin naming infants with surnames
for taxation, draft, and education, in addition to their formal Hebrew names "son of so-and-so," "daughter of so-and-so," many Jews
regarded the edict to use surnames with skepticism, a surname
scant protection for a stateless Jew. After 1844, some Jewish men of
conscription age in Volyn Province changed their surnames often,
thinking that by doing so they could outsmart Sad Angel and the
death sentence of a long conscription in the tsar's army.

The Hebrew letter *bet* and the Hebrew letter *peh*, voiced (*bet*)
and unvoiced (*peh*) consonants, are easy to mishear, like *b* and *v*
in English. In hurried handwriting, the *bet* and *peh* look similar,
one with a curved bottom, one an oval. Looking for the surname
Plat before Sad Angel comes swooping down prematurely is a tricky
proposition. Could there be a scrap of paper in the ephemera collected in the *Pinkas* book of Ratne, a hodgepodge of history, business transactions—who gave what tithe to the Great Yeshiva in Vilnius, how much so-and-so's milk cow sold for in 1853? Esta Plat,
entrepreneur, exporter of forest mushrooms, taxes leveed in 1932
and paid in full at the county seat in Lutsk? A fool's errand record
like that, a small victory over Sad Angel's complete obliteration?

In Kieślowski's film, when Weronika suffers a heart attack, Véronique winces and clutches her aching chest. When Esta Plat attempted to outrun the bayonet on the tip of the rifle of the *Ein-*

satzgruppe commando urging her forward to the pit on the edge of the Prokhid Hills, Sad Angel sent a stab between my grandmother's scapula that knocked her to her knees. She thought the grief she felt was worry for her husband's failing health, though he hadn't yet been diagnosed with pancreatic cancer. When she heard the scrape of a shovel head against hardpan, her neighbor Mrs. Schwartz trying to dig her way back to Ratne from Newton Street on the west side of Denver, the sound of scraping metal brought my grandmother's hands to her ears, as though the dirt piled on top of Esta's splintered skull was being shoveled onto hers.

In the *Rocky Mountain Jewish News*, on March 29, 1945, the headline asked, "What Happened to Polish Jewry? Only 30,000 Are Still Alive." Before she forgot everything, my grandmother's neighbor, Mrs. Schwartz, knew the answer to the paper's question. That is why Mrs. Schwartz dug and dug, back to her imagined childhood garden of beets and cabbages before the Jew apocalypse.

Dear Susha,

The militia entered Ratno and all the bees flew off. My grandson said, "Bubbie, look at the big fish hanging in the plum tree in the yard!" like the sturgeon your father caught when your brother Ben was born. I went outside, and ten thousand bees clung to one another as they surrounded their queen to fly her through the sky. I wish the bees would cover me and fly me somewhere safe. When I close my eyes, it's 1920 again, when Bałachowicz's butchers dragged one hundred families from their homes and shot them all. The mutilations, well, you know.

I spit on them. I spit on White Russians. I spit on Cossacks. I spit on Bolsheviks. I have spit on so many Jew haters I have no spittle left. I waved alongside my man when the Poles paraded down the street and claimed Ratno as their territory, reclaiming what was "theirs." For two years after, they murdered us. It's a miracle my arm didn't fall off from so much waving.

———

Honey was considered rustic, the provenance of Old World bubbies, too flavorful, unrefined, and a carrier of microbial diseases
when raw. My mother preferred white sugar, yet Susha stockpiled
gallon jars of honey in the pantry in her cellar, more jars than she
would ever use.

Cronson, singulare tantum, was a honey-laden pastry I like to
think Susha named in concert with Esta Plat, to lend their kitchens an intracontinental flair. *Cronson* did not commemorate side-
stepping genocide as hamantaschen did on Purim; the pastry was
served to usher in the new year. Had the records been extant, letters
might have floated back and forth across the Atlantic while Susha
and Esta bandied nomenclature. Susha would describe her streetcar rides down West Colfax Avenue to downtown Denver, and in
one letter she would have slipped a photo of herself in a tight black
rayon dress patterned with white chevrons. Not recorded by the
camera, nylon stockings with seams running up the backs of her
thick calves. She was on her way downtown to eat unkosher croissants with her eldest daughter, Evelyn.

In return, Esta Plat would have sent a photo of herself in a party
dress she borrowed from her daughter-in-law, off the shoulder
sleeves, too tight across the tuches, yellow, though you can't see the
color in a photo. She wore the dress during the homecoming celebration of Ratners returning from Buenos Aires to spread the word
about the good life awaiting Jews in Argentina, if only they would
take the chance and flee.

We were so careful about God's laws, Susha might have said.

He isn't watching, Esta might have replied. *Live it up.*

Though croissants are crescent shaped, fine, and flaky when
rolled with a practiced hand, Susha's *cronson* resembled fat, three-
inch cigars filled with minced walnuts mixed with cinnamon and
honey. They weren't pretty or dainty, light, flaky, or buttery. They
contained neither cream cheese, butter, nor milk, and their texture
did not resemble the flaky dough in rugelach. *Cronson* were sub-

stantial the way a heavy sweet roll is, lolling in the pit of the stomach as a ball of undigested batter, just smaller, and always pareve, neither meat nor dairy. The pastry resembled the dough for hamantaschen, but the corn oil–infused dough of *cronson* was tough like overworked pie crust or undercooked strudel without the apples.

By the time I asked my grandmother for her recipe for *cronson*, Sad Angel had already made its third sweep across her mind. She didn't know what honey was or why it was so sticky, and she didn't like the taste. I have found no recipes for *cronson* in eastern European cookbooks of any ethnic group. *Cronson* only obliquely look, taste, and smell like croissants, but the pronunciation of *croissant* in Ukrainian sounds very similar to *cronson*: kru-á-san. Kru-á-san, *cronson*. An inside joke between two dear friends who seldom laughed together.

Take that, Sad Angel.

Shoahtecture I

T HE ARTIFICIAL SWALES IN THE PROKHID HILLS outside of Ratne are eroded mass graves caving in. Among the pits, Prokhid's sandy hills support a quarry and a sand lot whose contents have been mined, scooped, and sifted to pick out human bones. Eroded and plundered since 1942, a forest has encroached on the deepest, steepest pits. For almost seventy years since then, sand from the quarry site was mixed into cement for blocks and barricades, like the broken tombstones from vandalized Jewish cemeteries throughout Europe repurposed into curbs and paving stones. In 1995, Ratners who had resettled in Israel erected a memorial stone to Ratne's murdered Jews more demure and streamlined than the stone at the western edge of Synagogenplatz in Ludwigsburg.

Human bones are strewn throughout the hills like the silver wrappers smeared with tzatziki sauce from *döner* kebabs tossed inside the gravel perimeter of what was once the synagogue sanctuary in Ludwigsburg. Carnivorous mammals and birds continue to transform the bones, tearing and pecking, gnawing on the afterthoughts of femurs as they would at carcasses of hedgehogs, fox,

chickadees, or voles, drawn by echoes of high-pitched trills suspended in a branch, cartilage from a knee that left an impression of
a curve in sand.

See there? In the crook of that tree? A crow dropped Esta's humming jawbone when it was struck by another crow, no appetite for
human jaw without its gums and blood, just curious, envious as a
Cossack who murdered for a candelabra made from tin.

What glint caught the crow's attention? No glint. As the jawbone struck the forest duff, tinny notes like a comb's metal teeth
striking the drum of a music box announced a shovel's blade.

The largest grave pit in the Prokhid Hills was sealed in September 2011 with the labor of Maurice Herszaft in a memorial project organized by the American Jewish Committee, Berlin. By 2014,
three more mass graves filled with Jews after their slaughter in August 1942 were likewise sealed and incorporated into the design
footprint of the Prokhid Hills memorial site, rededicated in 2015
by Rabbi Mordechai Bald of Lviv. Seventy-two years after Jews were
massacred in Ratne, sand excavation in the Prokhid Hills was also
halted.

Mine is not a clan conversant in Shoahtecture shrines. Susha's
dining room buffet on Newton Street boasted a samovar, an awk-
ward relic of curlicues and braided silver from the time before. If
beads of moisture like a sweating human brow coated the silver-
plated surface of the samovar when Esta died, or after, for the week
Esta Plat's shiva would have been observed, if a flock of invasive
Eurasian doves cooed on the fence outside the window, who among
the clan would allow themselves to read the signs?

In the drawer directly underneath the samovar, Susha's tzeda-
kah charity tins for Hadassah, Linas Hatzedek, Bikur Cholim, and
the Hebrew Educational Alliance occupied a third of the space, the
other two-thirds black rayon yarmulkes and blue-and-white Max-
well House coffee Haggadahs. On top of her china cabinet, a pair
of hand-carved figurines of a stooped Old Country zayde and a

stooped Old Country bubbie loomed over Susha's midcentury family gathered at her table, figurines gifted by aunties after their visit to Jerusalem in the early 1960s. Peasants, down to his knee-high boots and her plain babushka covering all her wooden hair, day and night the figures stood bowing to each other and Hashem, Denver's arid climate leaching them of color, sucking out their pith as they silently judged everyone for their ersatz piety and their patina of respect coating a past they wished they didn't own. Susha's beloved RCA radio in its hardwood cabinet was directly opposite, the mesh over its speakers vibrating like hummingbird wings, its dials and face plate high as heaven to the little girl I was, strains of Lawrence Welk's accordion playing polkas no one could dance to anymore.

Buffalo Bill Cody's grave in Lookout Mountain park and a twenty-two-foot-high Mother Cabrini gracing the foothills west of Denver had nothing over the gothic monoliths for my ancestors in the Rose Hill Cemetery. The austere white marker for Susha's first child, Anne, is in the cemetery's sinking first section, many stones nearly gone back into the ground, Anne nearly effaced from the family's memory, excluded from Susha's borne-child list, as was the custom for forgetting deceased children not swept along into the insistent current of a fuller life.

But nothing in these shrines or on these family gravestones carved in deliberate, relative calm could compare to architectural intention, the fractured lines and dead-end paths at the Prokhid Hills memorial, strewn prismatic angles longing to reconfigure in a Star of David that still means hope and faith, a menorah carved in stone extinguished and always burning, an info-stele half-apologizing to a universal God for how humanity turns feral.

Feasts

A DUKE OF WÜRTTEMBERG, WHEN YOUNG, WAS smitten by our friend Heide's unstudied beauty, her frame unbent by wartime dairy rations. Her mahogany-colored hair shone, coaxed by a thousand caring strokes, and her voice was plaintive as an owl's. One day the duke's chauffeur arrived to present Heide with a ring-necked pheasant recently harvested from the duke's private, stocked reserve on hunting grounds that stretched from the royal stud farm in Stuttgart to the royal hunting grounds once abutting Favoritepark in Ludwigsburg.

The duke's chauffeur likely waited at the Brudis' threshold, grasping the inverted bird by its legs. It's not every day a woman is gifted a dead pheasant from the duke's estate, so Heide thanked the chauffeur and took the pheasant to her tiny kitchen and rummaged in the cupboard to find a bag in which to pluck the bronze and sable feathers. Could she recollect watching her grandfather pluck and draw a pheasant? Had he? That time was so removed from this, piles of broken glass and bombed out, twisted metal still visible in a rubbish mound outside her city. The gift seemed ludicrous, cruel perhaps, harkening the exclusive, excessive, deadly aristocratic past, the traces of it, its implacable arrogance. Its resilience. Its insistence. Its survival. She'd survived by learning how to view time as though it were a series of marks on a slide rule, the more distant, linear past superseded by the more recent on a logarithmic scale, represented as a curve, not unlike the curved breast of the well-fed, half-plucked bird now sprawling on her counter.

Trying not to tear the thin breast skin as she ripped out feathers, she then flipped the bird and cleared the back, pulling feathers up from the thighs to the pheasant's head. Her cooking shears were dull, but she cut and yanked at joints of the outer wings and feet, used a hastily, not all together sharpened knife to cut the neck close to the start of the pheasant's tippet feathers. The geese she'd helped to roast for Christmas *Weihnachtsgans* were nothing like this bird, this beauty, this captive, game-park pet. One deliberate thwack and its head fell to the floor, its beak clicking like a cheap cigarette lighter. Its marmite-colored eyes did not bewitch her; above the bird a subtle odor lingered, reminiscent of a cut whose scab falls off before the skin is healed. How to draw its entrails? The butcher had always gutted the family's Christmas goose.

A chef can stick her forefinger up a pheasant's vent, the anus, to begin to gut the bird, rotate the finger to loosen the entrails, add the middle finger, pull. More delicate would be to cut around the vent, taking care not to puncture it, remove the excess skin to create a larger area in which to work, rotate the middle and forefinger around inside the bird to loosen entrails, pull. In theory, especially if the chef's fingers are strong, all the entrails spill out in one or two pulls. There is a chance the intestines could tear, and there is a chance that the gizzard sack, full of undigested particles, could also tear and empty its contents inside the bird's cavity—gravel, sand, hard seeds, spiders, a variety of forbs—if not sullying the carcass, then introducing the flavors of undigested fiber that one wild pheasant hunter described as moldy salsa mixed with rusty drain pipe flakes.

Cooking instructions on how to prepare a wild pheasant say to simply wash the pheasant cavity thoroughly if a tear and spill occur, because, who wants to throw away a pheasant shot by a duke, or any lucky hunter? Besides, preparations for cooking the bird should mask the rusty taste—skin rubbed with hazelnut oil, rosemary, and sage, the bird's cavity stuffed with chanterelles, other dried forest mushrooms from eastern Europe like the ones Esta Plat once exported, shallots, and roasted barley, the legs trussed tightly with cooking twine for a handsome presentation.

Heide roasted the pheasant deep brown, her small apartment filled with the aroma of gamey bird, presented the fowl atop the family's silver on a bed of cress surrounded by ruffles of Italian parsley. Walter Brudi and his wife had been invited to the feast, and Christoph winked at Heide as he ignored his father's directions to start the serving cut lower on the breast. Christoph sliced high, near where the start of the bird's crop would have been. Essence of mulch escaped the cut, old compost, river mud, beetles, as the diners discreetly tried to ignore the odors. Christoph's knife hovered above the bird like a divining rod, then alighted on the already severed legs, farthest from the pheasant's gizzard, but by then, the diners had lost their appetites.

The Bavarian artist Theo Scharf, like Christoph's father, was a Kriegsmaler from 1940 to 1945, and the pulsating yellow petals of Ukrainian sunflowers caught his eye. In one account of his tenure as a war artist, written after the 1941 battle over the town of Maheriv, Scharf observed the dust collecting on a fallen Russian soldier's corpse, around it bloated, dead horses, while in the middle distance corncobs in the fields swelled and ripened. Scharf rhapsodized about how delicious the butter-colored kernels tasted as he downed them during the Battle of Uman in 1941.

Scharf was transferred to Berlin-Potsdam to work in a propaganda unit called Staffel der Bildenden Künstler, Artists' Squadron, assigned first to Norway in 1943, to sketch typical pastoral Norwegian scenes like fishing and hunting pheasants as studies for the murals he would have painted after Norway's annexation to Germany.

June 1943 in Grabówka, Esther Nisenthal Krinitz, a fabric artist, was weeding the strawberry patch belonging to the Polish farmer sheltering her. She'd fled from Nazi soldiers and told the old farmer who protected her she was a Polish Catholic farm girl, and whether he believed her or not, he took her in to be his housekeeper. North of the strawberry patch, between a pathway and an orchard of apple, pear, cherry, and plum trees, the farmer had several beehives, and the bees were gathering pollen in the sun as Esther filled her basket with strawberries. Two Nazi soldiers entered the garden and trampled the farmer's cabbage patch senselessly, maliciously, carelessly, even though everyone felt the scarcity of food in 1943. Even the soldiers' own belts were two punch-holes tighter. When they saw fecund Esther kneeling in the strawberries with her thick red braids wound atop her head, and with juicy red berries in her basket, one aimed his rifle at Esther's head.

"Click," he said, and laughed.

The farmer leaning on his cane in the farmhouse doorway stiffened in horror, unable to defend himself, or Esther, from the soldiers. Rape was not a stranger to any woman, girl, or toddler, so Esther kept her head down and wrapped her forefinger around a ripe berry to pull it off the stem, and when the fruit complied, every nerve ending in her body exploded. She pulled weeds around the plants' bundles slowly, slowly tore ripe berries from their stems so that the bees wouldn't buzz around her face and sting her. From the corner of her right eye, she watched the closest soldier's rifle stock. She'd seen her grandfather beaten senseless by two Nazi soldiers' rifle stocks, her parents, brother, and younger sister loaded at rifle point onto a cart heading toward the Kraśnik railroad station and on to death in Majdanek.

The stench of caked, dried semen, pus, and menstrual blood in the soldiers' pants revolted bees, and they swarmed around the soldiers' heads and stung them on their ears, eyelids, inside their nostrils, on their lips, cheeks, and tongues, on the napes of their necks and their Adam's apples. Each attacking honeybee sacrificed itself, digging its hooked barb deep, as bees do to protect their queen.

"You cunt!" the soldiers screamed as they fled the yard, "Why aren't you being stung like us?"

But Esther had been stung, with a million stings of grief. The butt of a German rifle crashed against her skull when she didn't move quickly enough to vacate her family's home, but it hadn't killed or maimed her. After she escaped with her younger sister, all their hiding places were discovered as they fled from village to village, each of her parents' friends betraying her for the bounty they collected for turning in a pair of filthy, worthless Jews.

Esther's artistic eye remembered not the dust on a Russian soldier's corpse, not a bloated horse, but the rapist soldiers' white-knuckled fists and how they clasped their rifles. She remembered how the sun sparkled off the bullet casings aligned in rows on their bandoliers. One took off his hat to wave away the bees, which provoked bees to sting him more. She remembered his matted blond hair and how it looked like dirty straw that horses had shat on in a stable she once cleaned.

The scene Esther depicts in her fabric collage is orderly and lush, and she is about to pivot as the soldiers turn to rape her. Purple wisteria grows against the farmer's house, and red hollyhocks blossom in his garden. The farmstead aches with life. Each tree in the orchard is laden with blossoms, and cherry boughs bend, heavy with fruit. Esther's strawberry basket is piled past the brim, yet no berries spill. The Nazi soldiers intrude like white-face killer clowns, each soldier with his bandolier, depicted as five bullets around one man's waist, six around the other, the bullets large enough to fell a bear or shatter every bone, tooth, and atom of a teenage girl.

———————

Dusk has never been my favorite time of day. I learned of my grandmother's death at dusk, my father's, my mother's, and late-fall dusk in southern Germany, especially, conjures the threat of Chernobyl radiation still steeping in the atmosphere, underground, in the claws of feral cats and in the tiny blood-spot hearts of fertile chicken eggs. The odor of desiccating mushrooms in Favoritepark nearby intensifies at dusk, sewer stink, foul shadows of men that may or may not menace. A late-autumn chill rising off the cultivated fields that ring Ludwigsburg seeps into the marrow.

While working in Ludwigsburg alone in late autumn 2014, I forced myself to amble every day at dusk and into dark, to extend the day and shorten the awful length of night. I walked in a circle around the university, starting at the far northern edge of the Favoritepark fence at the roundabout on Reuteallee, then along the asphalt path, where I often saw a wary hare bounding into or out of the woods on the university's edge, until the woods, defined by a tangle of blackberry vines and young birch suckers, were cut to the ground just before American Thanksgiving making what was once hidden visible.

Another woman walked a parallel circuit to mine, starting inside Favoritepark before the gates locked at dusk, and we often passed one another near the stone lions in front of the Chinese restaurant on Neckarstraße. Our wan smiles marked our recognition of one another, though we never spoke or learned each other's names. A few times I'd seen one of my students riding his bicycle, his guitar case strapped across his back, once a grandmother angrily lecturing her grandchild as the boy pressed his hands tightly to his ears. Most of the time alone, I thought how the bramble-covered ditch across the street from my faculty guest apartment would be a good place to toss a corpse.

At the culmination of my walk, if I succeeded in greeting at least one gloomy fellow in the gloomy dusk, I would treat myself to

Hähnchengrill, salty, rotisserie-fired hens I bought at the food truck parked across the street from a small convenience store called Nah und Gut near the university's west side parking lot.

The salty food bloated me for days, but the discomfort was nothing compared to that of the chickens, grown in shoebox-sized cages in dark Quonset-style warehouses, butchered, plucked, eviscerated by machine, then arranged on skewers seven lines high in heart-opening pose to be blasted in the heat. If there was a long line at the food truck, it would be completely dark once I approached the un-lit carport at the entrance to my flat, canceling out any semblance of well-being I might have mustered as I chanted *Keinehora, Keinehora* with every step, to ward off the evil eye.

The man who sold hähnchengrill in his food truck smiled and lifted his chin as I approached, dropped the gray rag he used to wipe his counter between orders. He turned, looked back over his shoulder as he pointed to the top rack of the glossy roasted hens with sweaty breasts, and unhooked the metal clasp that held a line of hens rigid on a skewer. Hen on the counter, he'd grab his clever and thwack the bird in two. Though I always ordered half a hen from his tiny menu, he'd hesitate for a minute before he wrapped the bird in silver paper, as if waiting for the rest of my order, so I could demonstrate, I thought, that I did not dine alone.

When a larger order didn't come, he'd stuff a napkin, a cellophane-wrapped towelette, and one breath mint along with the cleaved chicken in a paper bag. We said very little to one another, "a hen," "yes, cut in half," "thank you very much," "I have the correct change today," and then I would turn away and walk back to my apartment with my warm package beginning to seep out grease. Before I went inside, I'd check the bird feeder on the hook above the back stoop to see if the finches and chickadees had eaten all the seed, then light the votive candles I had placed on the window ledge next to blossoming red Christmas cacti. I did not feel Scandinavian hygge or Norwegian *koselig* cheer; if anything, I prayed to the great whomever that I wouldn't get salmonella poisoning from the anus of an industrial hen shitting in proximity to its cagemates.

On the Tuesday the vendor and his truck were missing, I asked about him at the Nah und Gut corner grocery across the street from where the vendor parked. It was an overcast day, and everyone in the store was dressed to match the sky or mud and seemed to be suffering from tooth pain. The woman behind the counter of the small bakery in the front of the store shook her hands, but I couldn't tell whether she was irritated by my question, or the vendor, his competition with the grocery, couldn't understand me, or was just generally annoyed. I settled on the latter explanation. It had been raining off and on all day and people including me had tracked mud mixed with sand from nearby cobblestones all over the front of the store, smeared the storefront window when they leaned their wet umbrellas up against the glass. She said she didn't know what or whom I meant when I pointed across the street. Another customer bumped me from behind as she butted to the front of the line to purchase the last five mixed-seed rolls from the baker's case, two of which I had hoped to buy myself. The cashier in the grocery line was chewing out a customer for not tossing his recycled plastic sparkling water bottles into the receptacle fast enough, and two Croatian workmen behind their buddy were laughing at her pique.

It was a very unwelcoming gathering at dusk, everyone establishing their immigrant pecking order—the bakery clerk with her dyed red hair and cigarette breath counting the minutes until she could close her station and sweep bread crumbs into her dirty red dustpan, the Croatian bricklayers who were building a high-end duplex next to the field of oats on the edge of Favoritepark and were in the grocery that evening for their customary after-work six-packs of beer, the cashier of indeterminate origin who sighed each time she was interrupted from reading her movie magazine or cleaning the dirt out of her long, blue-lacquered fingernails in order to ring up the grocery orders of her customers. I forgot the word for *matches*, which were lodged behind the checkout counter. The cashier had to retrieve them, and so I said "fire sticks," mimed lighting a cigarette, which should have provoked at least a chuckle, but didn't.

The next Tuesday, the hähnchengrill vendor was back, standing in his food truck, the aroma of salty rotisserie chicken wafting down the street. He wore a different jacket, light beige cotton, and he looked even skinnier than before. There was a scabbed-over cut in the corner of his mouth. His gray hair, usually parted with precision and combed until every strand was plastered to his head, looked tousled, as though he'd just been in a row. He spoke Turkish in an urgent whisper to someone on his cell phone and seemed harried by his rush of customers buying up their dinners before they disappeared into their cars or the apartments in the blocks nearby. His line grew longer still, and as he spoke, the cut on his mouth opened and bled onto his teeth, his mouth pinched in pained obsequiousness as he stammered, trying to make small talk with German native speakers. One giant of a man grew irritated when the vendor asked him to repeat his order, and the customer grabbed the illustrated laminated menu on the countertop and punched at the photographs of fried potatoes and chicken parts in various configurations of quantity and cut. The customer thrummed his knuckles on the counter while he waited, flipped his cell phone lid up and down, and when his order was ready, he tossed several euro coins on the counter as though into a beggar's cup. He grabbed his big white bag of roasted chickens and potatoes and sped off in his tricked-out racing-yellow Porsche.

A young mother with her two children stepped up to the counter next, ordered a hen and french fries for her family by shyly pointing to a glossy picture plastered on the front of the vendor's truck. The man held up three fingers, three grilled hens, to which the mother shook her head slowly, sadly, and held up one finger only. All three of them were dressed for Arctic weather, the mother in a thick, heavy gray wool coat, with a black wool scarf decorated with red roses tied under her chin. The zippers were broken on the children's quilted parkas, and the boy and girl wore hand-knitted hats and heavy mittens. All of them wore insulated snow pants tucked into knee-length rubber boots, even though the day was balmy in spite of rain. The children were dirty after playing in wet sand on the playground a block from the vendor's truck, and the little boy carried a green plastic bucket with two little shovels the children had used to build the foundation for their Pyramid of Giza. The girl's hat was peppered with sand, and the boy's mittens were caked. Their faces seemed not to have been washed since breakfast time.

The vendor looked down at them, and at their mother, whose coat was sandy too, as though she'd been at a beach and let her children bury her in sand. The man mumbled a question to her in simple German, but she didn't understand. He shrugged his shoulders, shook his head, and smiled. He had a gold tooth, the first and last time I saw it.

The boy became more interested in the dinner transaction as the vendor fumbled with something under his counter while the basket of frying potatoes behind him was splattering hot oil. The vendor retrieved two ancient suckers whose clear wrappers looked like they might crumble if handled without care. Each of the red candies was cracked across the center, and the sticks, once straight and rigid, were softened, bent. The boy put down his green plastic bucket. Both children, wide-eyed, clapped their hands and consulted with their mother, whispering behind their mittens.

The woman turned her head toward Frankfurter Straße as a bus stopped to pick up passengers on the corner. When it departed, it sprayed a curtain of water on the windshield of the idling car behind it. The lights in the Mercedes-Benz showroom blinked then blazed the buff and polish of opulent, dark-colored cars, in answer to her gaze. The woman turned back to the vendor and nodded, and he leaned over the narrow counter and handed the suckers down to the children.

A few weeks later my husband had joined me in Ludwigsburg before we departed Germany so that I could search for traces of Esta Plat in archives in Jerusalem, and together we approached the hähnchengrill truck. We'd walked the circuit of my hygge dusk-extension together, but with my husband present, my solitary hygge practice now seemed brief and half-hearted, furtive, pathetic, really. If it were company I was after, gathering, being around other people, I'd chosen one of the most desolate paths in Ludwigsburg to skirt.

Dusk began to deepen into darkness. The elegant woman I often noticed beginning her stroll near the Chinese restaurant on Neckarstraße had not been present as she had been on many of my walks. My husband and I watched three couples in their fifties congregated in a field near the university tennis courts, across the street from the Lidl grocery outlet. As they chatted, clouds of breath rose from their lips, as their dogs sniffed and nipped at one another. The couples raised their arms, threw back their heads, and laughed, shook their hands and pointed their gloved fingers at their happy dogs. The obedient dogs twisted in tight circles close to the legs of their owners, but when the pets realized that they were free to roam, they bounded off to sniff and scratch in the dirt. The first red Frisbee appeared, and the dogs yelped and jumped in unison. One of the couples broke away and chased each other, but the woman tired quickly, and when the man caught her and leaned in for a kiss, she rummaged in her purse for a cigarette, which she lit and handed to her mate.

The chicken vendor grinned when he saw my husband standing with me in front of his food truck. I like to think the vendor felt relieved to see that I wouldn't be eating one cleaved half of a greasy little hen alone, one toothpick-sized drumstick, flightless wing, and half a breast. In fact, the vendor nodded and hummed a little tune when I ordered two whole chickens and enough french fries for the both of us.

Our German friends insist *Gemütlichkeit*, the German equivalent for hygge, is a slightly different concept than the Danes or Norwegians practice, gemütlichkeit embodying warmth but anticipating being cozily inside. Gathering and cheer, they say, implies an expectation of protection and solace in the home and the knowledge of how to seek it, taking care. One can experience gemütlichkeit alone, and should, if one lives alone.

The German Christmas market, *Weihnachtsmarkt*, for example, like the one in Ludwigsburg, has gemütlichkeit potential, attended by groups of raucous friends who engage in gemütlichkeit together. Friends help each other to achieve dollops of gemütlichkeit, as Susha and Esta did when they were girls in Ratne. Technically though, according to the nuance in the definition, standing under heat lamps eating grilled sausages and boar's collar and sipping glühwein fortified with brandy while bundled in a heavy winter coat anticipates gemütlichkeit, once one has exited the elements. It's not cozy, after all, to stand in the pouring rain or pelting sleet, even if you're eating pitted dates stuffed with almonds dipped in honey.

Another Set for
Brundibár

A FEW WEEKS AFTER THE AUTUMN FESTIVAL OF Sukkot several years ago, a kibbutznik on a fundraising tour for her collective came to my friend Rhonda's Hebrew school class. My parents had pulled my younger sister and me from that synagogue and Hebrew school two years prior, my father exercising his malaise, disgust, and disdain over the cost of dues, and my mother her exasperation over the gut gripes that struck me at exactly 3:00 p.m. every Monday and Wednesday right before our Hebrew school class began.

We had joined a nascent synagogue whose Hebrew school was held in mobile classrooms that smelled like formaldehyde and paint, the congregation waiting in limbo until trustees could raise the funds to move out of the white ranch-style house and adjoining trailers in which its congregants convened. It was in one of the forbidden trailers where I spied on bar mitzvah boys learning to wind phylacteries around their skinny arms, and where a few of us discovered our teacher, Mr. Waddell, hiding after John Kennedy was shot. Mr. Waddell's fists were clenched against his forehead like Susha clenched her fists, his violent weeping loud and uncontrolled, terrifying in its raw despair.

We were exposed to grief like that systematically, it seemed, as though we were a roll of undeveloped film made to bear witness to our inheritance frame by frame. My mother insisted it had something to do with being Jewish and knowing God, but what I knew was that if anyone glimpsed the cynic who crouched inside a chamber of my young heart, no gut gripes or any other kind of self-inflicted wound could save me from eternity in Sheol.

The kibbutznik stood in the middle of the circle formed around her, and to a one, the boys and girls thought they were going to play musical chairs, a welcome reprieve after yet another caution from the rabbi that petting was considered sex, followed by a useless recitation for all the sounds barnyard animals make in Hebrew. בה בה (*hav hav*), barked the little dogs.

I imagined the woman's body odors like a sprinter's, her breath like mackerel and red onions on stale challah, Susha's favorite lunch and also that of my first boss, Paul, whose family spent the war years hiding in Shanghai.

The woman's teeth were crooked, too gray seeming for her age. She had described her fieldwork as harvesting cucumbers in the desert sun, but her face was pale and luminous as a pearl. Her hands were small and silken, her manicured red nails long, the ugly silver pinkie ring encasing an Eilat stone polished and unscratched. Unlike the other guests from Israel, she didn't bring anything exotic like the palm frond (*lulav*) or citrus (*etrog*) necessary for the rituals of Sukkot, or hard candy that tasted like pomegranate seeds. She just brought her Azrael wings, put them on, and flapped.

Though they were only eleven, and years, they thought, from puberty, one boy with peach fuzz on his upper lip had to crouch so deeply his knees pressed up close to his shoulders as he struggled to remain on his little chair. As the woman contemplated Nina, a girl with messy, uneven braids, she rubbed her pointer finger back and forth across her lower lip, splitting it open further. The air in Denver is dry all year, but especially during the hot weeks before the weather changes in late October, which is why dining in a sukkah outdoors was so delicious. So many lips split and bled in Denver, everyone knew the salty taste of blood.

The woman removed her finger, licked the blood from the tip as though it were a dab of cookie batter, and continued examining Nina's thick black hair, her olive skin and hirsute arms, brown eyes, heavy lids and thick lashes, the dark circles underneath her eyes. The woman turned to regard each child briefly in this way, sniffing out those typical Jewish traits. They waited for a Hebrew ditty she might teach, like another guest who taught "*Zum Gali Gali*," with its line "and peace shall be for all the earth," but no song issued from the woman's lips. The large boy squirmed, and she flapped her wings to freeze him. She didn't repeat the children's names when the teacher provided them, as other visitors had, and she didn't say she was overjoyed to meet such strong and beautiful boys and girls, as all the other visitors from Israel did. If anything, she seemed bored.

The woman from Israel was short, though not as short as Susha, whose growth, she said, was stunted in the Old Country when her family ran out of food. Because of childhood deprivation, Susha's mission was to fatten as many of her relatives as she could, a battle, as it turned out, she did not win, even with her river of honey, schmaltz, and matzo meal, because my mother, all the aunties, and the cousins pursued the unattainable physiques of Norwegian cross-country skiers. Spirituality, religion, and Hashem became conflated with her production of latkes and applesauce, and the battles over too much strudel and industrial-sized sheets of honey cake overshadowed what it might mean, post-Shoah, to still believe in God.

When the Israeli woman had looked at each of the children long enough, she broke the circle apart by pushing on the shoulders of two of the smaller children to indicate that she wanted out, then she walked around the circle behind each child. Underneath her camel-colored skirt, her slip rubbed against the nubs of her garters, her leg hair matted under her nylon stockings. In other cir-

cumstances, the girls, at least, would have tittered about her anti-
quated hygiene, but something about the lice clinging to her Sad
Angel wings told the class she was dangerous, or her message was.

When is the right time to educate a child about betrayal, to
guide a child along the gauntlet of truth and myth, history on one
side and a land flowing with milk and honey on the other?

At exactly 4:00 p.m., the woman began tapping the right shoulder of many, many children. Tap, tap, and tap. She circled around
the group twice more, stopped behind Rhonda, and breathed heav-
ily on her neck, then slapped her on the shoulder, too.

Because they were seated in a circle, the children could see who
was tapped and who wasn't. The Israeli woman could see the aftermath of her taps on faces—smirks, bravado, fear—as she wielded
her taps like a scythe through a field of corn. The room filled with
shy, asthmatic snorts and rattles, hiccups, a muffled, musty fart no
one jubilantly accused his chum of cutting, the scratch of pencil
on paper as the teacher sat at his desk correcting math homework
from his day job. The odor of the sweet but slightly acidic sweat of
children, the sugars in licorice breaking down behind their braces,
the moth-wing smell of the ones who hadn't washed their hair for a
week mingled with the dusty air.

"Stand," she said.

Confused, they looked from one to the other. Which ones?

"Stand," the woman from Israel said again, "the ones I tapped.

"You!" she said, hardening her mouth as she stood in front of
seated Lynne, whose hands were folded atop the loden green dirndl
skirt her grandmother brought her back from Switzerland. "I
tapped you. Stand up."

Many children stood. Most. All but two. Both boys.

The woman glanced at the clock mounted above the door, 4:15.
Fifteen minutes until the children were free to run away. She didn't
explain the concept of her game, or if it had any rules, yet no one
told her that they'd wanted to play musical chairs instead. No one
challenged her to articulate the game plan.

Because she was from Israel, everyone assumed the woman was teaching them a lesson about pity. About how there is none. That was the lesson I recall learning about Israel in the early 1960s, how along with the miracle of its existence, it struggled to become as garish, cruel, racist, and violent as the United States was becoming. Became. Is. God didn't seem to be an essential part of it, though people pretended otherwise.

"You!" the woman said, pointing to seated Adam, his splayed hands pressing against his cheeks as he tried to hide a rash of pimples on both cheeks. "I missed you the first time. You're too short by inches. Stand up. See that Goliath over there on that pathetic little chair? Him, they would have kept to work to death."

Their teacher peeled back the silver foil from his roll of Tums. Usually, he downed half a roll then counted to ten aloud before he threw chalk or the eraser to express displeasure with his charges, at least to twenty before grabbing someone by the collar and accidentally bumping their heads on the doorjamb on their way to the hall. Susha, too, ate Tums like candy, before she went to shul on Saturdays, where she had to sit upstairs in the heat, sequestered in the women's section behind a blue velveteen curtain that sorely needed cleaning. I suspect now that all the sanctimony that substituted for devotion got to her, but I was never fluent in her one true language.

The woman ran her tongue over her lower lip. That was my habit too, even when my mother rubbed that nasty zinc oxide on my lips to keep me from licking them. The zinc oxide tasted better, I have to say, than the soap my mother used to wash my mouth out when I suggested God didn't care about our prayers.

When the woman from Israel finally turned away, her heels left faint scuff marks on the floor, tokens of her visit in case the class forgot. On her way out, she grabbed the tin box she'd passed around the circle for our spare change contributions to her kibbutz. No one said goodbye to her, because according to her demonstration, everyone but Goliath and another boy was dead. She'd delivered her quick lesson: there was no correlation between God and Hitler,

God and Stalin, God and political assassinations, God and mercy. God?! Better to harvest cucumbers in a field and sit around a camp-fire telling dirty jokes.

I had to say something heartfelt about God and faith at my con-firmation a few years later, and though my speech was a chastise-ment of those who turned to God only in times of need, I am one of those people. I knew God cared not about the misery and jealous wickedness we inflict on one another. By the time I was confirmed, Susha's honey was full of ants, her canister of matzah meal riddled with weevils, rancid nowhere near accurate in describing her jar of schmaltz. She spent her days in the Beth Israel Nursing Home knit-ting invisible sweaters with invisible needles for invisible Esta Plat. Nights, she ran along the slippery planks over the Pripyat swamp chasing Esta Plat, sweet Esta always there, always just beyond her reach.

What did that woman from Israel know that children wouldn't learn on their own? What gave her the right to pour the soured milk of history over the heads of children?

That's how things were done. Children needed to know there's plenty of rancid milk to go around that never turns to butter. Maybe that woman from Israel inherited the memory of her own grandmother, forced to tread water in a cesspool to save her life, and the woman from Israel couldn't put a cap on grief to let it go.

Out of 216,000 children deported to Auschwitz-Birkenau, 6,700 were selected to live and perform forced labor. One of those 6,700 was Malka Silberberg, the youngest sister of Rose Silberberg-Skier. Malka was three years old in 1942. In the last known photograph of Malka, she wore a plaid dress with short sleeves and a big bow on top of her head almost as broad as her brow. In better times, one might have joked that the bow made her look like a poodle. But when would those times be?

According to her sister Rose, Malka had a nightingale's voice, and so was lifted onto a table in front of a commander in Auschwitz and ordered to sing. Malka sang. When she completed her song, the commander lifted her down, his big hands in her little armpits, gave her a piece of hard candy, and sent her back to her barracks. The third time he summoned her, while she was singing to him on top of the table, he arose, walked behind her, drew his revolver, and put a bullet through the back of her skull. Standing from behind, he didn't dirty his uniform or see Malka's eyes as he shot her.

Like the commander, I wouldn't have wanted to watch that execution. Like him, I would have wanted to believe that I was doing something horrid, but necessarily merciful. That way, I could remain pragmatic, unsullied, righteous, maybe even blessed. If things went south, I could sign my name to open letters outlining the virtues of capitulation and the need for peace at any cost. The anecdote, recorded by The USC Shoah Foundation, doesn't say whether the commander believed in God, but I'm pretty sure he didn't put much purchase in Hashem. If he'd read the *Pirkei Avot, Ethics of Our Ancestors*, "Say little and do much" would have fit him to a tee.

During countless mountain hikes and bike rides around the Grande Ronde Valley with historian Nicole Howard, we spoke about the aggregate scrapbooks of the dead. If the dead have names, they live in historical accounts, even if only in a footnote, but what of the names said aloud, held aloft or hidden by the shame of recollection?

While searching one Mother's Day with Nicole and several others for the season's first morels, she paraphrased a passage from W. G. Sebald's *Austerlitz*, about how one remembers a certain view of a historical event, or if the event is complex and ongoing, the view coalesces, encapsulated by overlapping gestures, like Galena P— wadding up someone else's handkerchief while a penitent on Yom Kippur strikes his lips with a needle-studded apple, like a melody that holds equal beats with Adonai and Majdanek. Sebald implies that all of our memories of history, lived and imagined, are set pieces, reduced to a moment or an image, like Malka's execution. The set piece doesn't always list a cast.

There we were again, Nicole and I, mucking through the past while our husbands, children, friends filled baskets with bushels of morels from a fungal colony that stretched underground for miles. Life inserted itself into the never-static past, just as the children in the mock-Holocaust demonstration by the kibbutznik from Israel went home to supper with an extra stick of cherry-flavored licorice their teacher gifted them after class along with their new knowledge of Before.

Is it any less gruesome, knowing the fate of so many wartime children, then or now, to recall the paintings in primary colors of the children interned in Theresienstadt who studied art with interned Bauhaus artist Friedl Dicker-Brandeis before they were sent away, like Malka, to their deaths in Auschwitz? The children's set for the opera *Brundibár*, which they performed in Theresienstadt fifty-five times, might have seemed a rendition, as Maurice Sendak illustrated in his children's book *Brundibar*, a collaboration with Tony Kushner based on the play, of an attainable, idyllic town. Promenading gents and ladies in fur-trimmed cashmere coats tiptoed on a cobbled street with grand, tall churches and clock towers and even a modest synagogue, still standing. In the children's book, vendors' carts overflow with metal cannisters of milk and crocks of cheese and butter, loaves of bread and jam-filled pastries, emblems of a land of plenty. Is it any less gruesome to know that the child actors were given cakes and lemonade before they took the deathtrain east to Auschwitz? How much nicer it would be to replace Malka's doll-like face with fancy, forgetting that children always bear the brunt of war.

I watched *Ivan's Childhood* again, the first film of Russian filmmaker Andrei Tarkovsky, Ivan the brave boy who slips behind German lines close to the end of the war before the Russian army stormed Berlin after Hitler's suicide. Ivan was so frail and gangly, pale and blond, in the film's dream sequences so determined to carry out the pleas for vengeance scrawled on the wall of the bombed church where he is reunited with his protector, Captain Kholin. In the film's last dream sequence, after viewers learn from dossiers left at the prison that Ivan has been hanged by the Germans, after we've seen an image of the guillotine and the row of six hangman's nooses suspended from the ceiling in the prison yard in Berlin, we see Ivan as a shirtless boy running along the bank of a river, chasing his little sister, who also has no shirt on. She looks to be six or seven, happy, healthy. It seems as though he's trying to catch her or to tag her, but he reaches her and passes, as if they had been running a foot race after all, first along a sandbar in the water and then seemingly on the surface of the water. Water splashes up from Ivan's feet and long, sinewy legs as he runs above the water along a corridor of grace.

The USC Shoah Foundation interview of Rose Silberberg-Skier concluded with another photo. Rose spent 1942 to 1944 hiding among the chickens in a chicken coop in Sosnowiec, Poland, burrowed deep in shit and straw. Around the time Poland joined the European Union, Mrs. Stanisława Cicha sent Rose a photograph of the house in front of the chicken coop in which she hid, and on the back of the photograph, Mrs. Cicha wrote, "This is the house where we lived together during very hard times." Rose held the photo close to the interviewer's camera, but the chicken coop isn't visible. The photo shows the facade of what looks to be a good-sized wooden house.

Augury

A FRIEND CONFIDED THAT HE'D SMOKED HIS MOTH-er's ashes. He'd stored them in a porcelain urn, and her second incineration was born of his imagined desperation. He was lukewarm about his mother while she lived. He didn't have enough hashish left to fill his pipe, he'd said, so he topped off the bowl with his mother. He hadn't tried smoking her before, so he was surprised by the infinitesimal bits of bone fragment mixed with ashier cremains. He said as he rubbed a dab of ash between his fingers he thought of glass and how he might collect enough particles of bone, like the bits of quartz in Middle Eastern sand that Jews sprinkle atop caskets before interment. Then, he could forge a miniature smoked ellipse of Claude glass from his mother, slightly convex, the size of a postage stamp he could carry in the breast pocket of his favorite shirt, always looking backward over his shoulder, the way landscape artists in the nineteenth century shrank and abstracted what they would eventually paint.

The ash had the same consistency and feel as the powder his mother had used to dull the shine on the bridge and tip of her nose, gray as the lint that collected underneath his bed. His mother had hated lint and her favorite saying was the German one "Work is love made visible" which she applied to thankless dusting.

There were no hallucinations attached to the high, he said, as there were when he mixed opium with hash, nothing like seeing his mother materialize from smoke as a young woman with cone-shaped tits and a teased up bouffant, wearing a pale pink organdy gown and downing gin martinis, nothing like watching his conception or seeing his mother flying without an airplane above the Florida Keys, dissolving into the red, white, and blue sparks of a Roman candle. A bird alighted briefly on the balcony railing outside his window while he smoked, and though the sound startled him and sparked a surge of paranoiac energy to jolt his heart, when he found the source of the noise, it was an invasive Eurasian dove with a black stripe on the back of its neck. The dove remained a dove and not an Apollonian emanation of his mother.

I'd heard this friend confide the story about smoking his mother on more than one occasion, and each time a current of taboo rippled through the listeners, sometimes a large ampere registering shock, revulsion, sometimes a mixed, vacillating reading. We were inventing a new world, we thought, or better yet, a paradigm. No Kaddish. Just smoke, just ash. As time passed, and veterans from Vietnam stopped showing up at parties with oily cubes of hash, and later still, when Afghan hash became rare, the story fell away entirely.

We record the dreams in which the dead appear to us, scrambling to recall the sagacity of their mumbles. My friend said his mother caressed the crown of his head in a dream, as she had in life when fever woke him up. She'd stroked a piece of blue silk across his brow, the starless dark around them growing milky in predawn light, and then he was sitting in her idling car at the drive-through window of Taco John's, waiting for the beef tacos she would pass across the front seat, the toasted shell, the browned beef, the few shreds of cheddar cheese arranged in a crosshatch, the day-old iceberg lettuce, and the salty, smoky sauce that was neither hot nor authentic. As her hand reached out across the seat, her elbow locked, the fingers of her gloveless hand a perfectly closed and pointed arrow. Behind her there was a domino line of mothers, grandmothers, mummy mothers unraveling their bandages thread by thread as they waited at the drive-through. He'd had this dream more than once, usually when a deadline loomed or when he ate serrano peppers too late in the evening.

I read an anecdote about Freud that reminded me of Esta Plat. According to Florian Illies in *1913: The Year before the Storm*, Freud liked to hike in the forest outside Vienna, wearing lederhosen, a green boiled wool jacket, and a *Gamsbart* perched atop his hat like a miniature broom's bristles gone akimbo. In this costume, he hunted forest mushrooms, charging out in front of everyone in his gathering party, and when he found a creamy, dome-shaped pileus, he'd toss his funny hat over it until his daughter Anna came near, then, blowing on a silver whistle, he'd summon her, and she'd lift his hat brim and place the mushroom in her wicker basket.

In the pine forests at home where we hunt for mushrooms, the duff smells at once wet and dry, loamy and decaying. Fresh, just erupted morels have little odor, but morels past their prime smell like sweat inside old ski gloves mixed with desiccated parsley. Fresh chanterelles smell like apricots, and the aroma of *Boletus edulis* conjures grilling steak, though they don't smell like grilling steak; they just taste good served up beside grilled meat.

The first time I heard Esta Plat's name I heard it in conjunction with mushrooms. I was describing a game of mushroom polo to my mother during a Sunday night phone conversation, how my family and I had ridden our bicycles slowly along Forest Service roads looking for the pitted crenulations in the cone-shaped pileus of morels.

"Oh," my mother said, "Esta Plat sent Bubbie mushrooms from the Old Country."

"When?" I said.
"Before," she said.

Do we crack jokes to diminish abhorrent acts?

There were jokes about the conditions of prisoners in the labor, prison, and extermination camps during World War II, so many jokes that Rudolph Herzog shuffled them into genres in *Dead Funny*—humor and persecution, humor and war, humor and annihilation, humor and National Socialism.

Question: How can you tell the difference between an optimistic Jew and a pessimistic Jew?

Answer: A pessimistic Jew lives in Israel. An optimistic Jew lies at the bottom of an ash pit.

There were large ash pits in Birkenau, annex to Auschwitz, close to the crematoria, whose dormers in the roofline were designed to conjure Bavarian village bakeries.

The weight of cremains varies according to the size of the deceased and whether a wooden casket was included in the cremation process. Averaging out the live-weight discrepancy between men and women, the cremains of a well-fed peacetime corpse weighs 5.3 pounds. The cremains weight of a small village of seven thousand individuals, such as my grandmother and Esta Plat's village of Ratne in Ukraine, Jews and non-Jews both, no wooden caskets included, would be 37,100 pounds, almost nineteen tons, the same weight as four Ford F-450s with a cord of firewood in the back of each pickup.

In 1943 in the death camp Majdanek, near Lublin, 211 kilometers from Ratne, crude gray cremains, not ground to a smokable product or a palatable powder like the delicate ivory in compacts, were shoveled off the floor of the crematorium and piled in mounds between the north end of the crematorium and the bottom of the knoll of the camp's cabbage patch. Germans who administered the camp and its crematorium ordered men to fill small metal canisters with cremains and sold the canisters to rural Poles nearby, claiming that the ashes were the cremains of their fathers who had been incinerated in Buchenwald.

At the edge of the woods just beyond the barbed wire fence surrounding Majdanek, and just a few months before the Russian army liberated it, seventeen thousand Jews were marched to the edge of a pit and massacred all in one day in November 1943. Had their bodies been fully cremated instead of desecrated and partially buried in rubble and dirt, their collective cremains would have weighed 954,000 pounds, 477 tons, a small dealership of Ford pickups sitting seductively, promisingly on the lot, waiting to be financed and driven down the road.

Question: How much did occupying commanders know about nutrition during wartime?

Answer: They were experts! Germans needed 2,500 calories a day, Poles 600, and Jews 150.

Theresienstadt was a detention camp where Europe's deported Jewish artists and musicians congregated along with wealthy Jews who "rented" comfortable lodgings in a concentration camp. According to Jana Renée Friesová in *Fortress of My Youth*, internees in Theresienstadt were fed a little better, and they were permitted packages from relatives—food items of five hundred grams several times a week. Recipes for bars and cakes filled with fatty meat circulated on the outside—how best to pack a dense amount of calories into cakes weighing five hundred grams.

In the propaganda documentary filmed by Theresienstadt internee Kurt Gerron in 1944, *The Führer Gives a City to the Jews*, he pans the camera on many shots of happy children eating. In one, a beautiful little girl holds a piece of buttered toast to her lips, the sheen of marmalade like a lightly frosted skating pond catching the delighted glimmer in her eye. In another, a dark-eyed boy takes a chocolate-coated madeleine from a platter stacked high with the cream-filled cakes, quickly, trying to restrain himself from snatching up as many as he could and stuff them in his mouth. The belly-aches after all this rich and foreign food were exquisite, but it didn't really matter, because almost all the children who had been in Gerron's film, including Gerron himself, were sent east to Auschwitz in one of eleven transports that left the camp when the cameras stopped shooting footage of Hitler's gift to Jews.

In the days when most people smoked, my mother rolled her father's cigarettes for him, and Uncle Ben always had a stogie in his mouth. Our pediatrician, Dr. Plattner, smoked a pipe while writing out prescriptions for erythromycin, and my father had a humidor with cherry-scented tobacco though he smoked unfiltered Camels. Ash fell freely from cigarette tips resting in thick glass ashtrays, and many pairs of my father's slacks were ruined by ash burn holes. When Yellowstone National Park burned in 1988, ash from that fire fell from the sky onto our car 586 miles away. *To ash* became a verb, though it never ever meant to smoke your mother.

It's not unusual to add wood ash to a garden to sweeten loam, along with vegetable compost to make clay soil lofty, and it is verifiable in many gardening manuals that compost makes a garden greener. The decomposed debris of cucumber peel, fennel, eggshells, coffee grounds, cherry pits and stems will improve the anchoring of soft, new roots. Carrots and garlic especially thrive in soil like this. Maple wood billets create more ash than tamarack or pine, and though black walnut smells like something that shouldn't be on fire, ashes are ashes. Dirt accepts whatever is mixed with it. Cosmonaut Volkovs, heirloom tomatoes from Ukraine, respond well to lofty soil amended with ash, but every gardener knows that too much ash, or too little, can turn the soil's pH too alkaline or acidic so that vegetables and fruits present as dwarfed, with added nodules, or with so much foliage the plant produces nothing but inedible leaves.

Cabbage, on the other hand, forgives. It grows in many soils. Green cabbage leaves are best for *prakas*, also called *holishkes*, Ukrainian sweet-and-sour stuffed cabbage rolls. The leaves should be broad and fresh, Dutch or Savoy cabbage, at least for American consumers. Russian cabbage rolls, *golubtsi*, with slightly different ingredients, got their name, "fake doves," from the peasant dish prepared to mimic minced and roasted squab, known to us as pigeons, that mid-eighteenth-century Russian aristocracy liked to eat.

Russian/Polish/Ukrainian Jews like Esta Plat and Susha ate prakas on the holiday Simchat Torah, to celebrate the conclusion of the yearlong Torah reading cycle about to begin again. Two prakas, stuffed and rolled like logs, resemble an opened Torah scroll with its two uneven cylinders.

Yaakov Plot, a kinsman of Esta's and Susha's, told a story about an unmarried midwife named Milke the Bobe, who gave the synagogue of the Stepiner Hasidim in her village a new Torah scroll to replace the old and frayed one. A new Torah is a precious gift, wedded to the synagogue like a bride, and the klezmer band that Milke the Bobe hired to play at the reception for the new Torah was a band from Ratne. The anecdote doesn't list the band members' names or say whether Esta Plat was among them, or if the band was weighted evenly with clarinets and fiddles, whether they had a concertina, hammered dulcimer, or a button accordion, but perhaps they played "A Hora mit Branfn" ("A Hora with Brandy") and fortified their dancing with a recipe for cherry brandy Susha shared with Esta Plat—equal parts brandy, sugar, and red-blushed Royal Ann cherries.

Esther Nisenthal Krinitz's family grew cabbages in their garden in Mniszek, near what is now Annapol, Poland, and in September 1939, her mother harvested the last cabbages from their garden to make prakas for Simchat Torah. Esther was twelve, and she'd been apprenticed to a dressmaker named Juszia for three years, learning not only to sew but also to embroider, crochet, and knit. Later, after she'd waded through fetid swamps, hidden with the help of a Polish Catholic farmer, she was saved from Nazi soldiers by a swarm of honeybees that descended on the soldiers' heads before the soldiers could rape her. She met and married her husband in a displaced persons camp in Germany. It was she who told about the cylinders of cremains sold by Nazis to Polish farmers as their loved ones, a story she heard when she toured Majdanek as a soldier in 1944. Later, after she opened a dress shop with her own designs in Brooklyn, she also created fabric collage squares that, like Claude glass, distilled her autobiography, *Memories of Survival*.

The green cotton cabbages in Esther Nisenthal Krinitz's collage *Maidanek* (Majdanek), completed in October 1995, are half the height of the Russian and Polish soldiers who stand guard along the corridor in front of the liberated empty barracks, crematorium, and gas chamber depicted on the fabric square. It's August 1944, and the camp has been evacuated and cleared of German soldiers. Recruit Esther stands at the gate in a canary yellow dress with two long red braids hitting at her waist. A guard opens the gate for her. She rummages through a huge mound of shoes taken from the feet of prisoners before they were incinerated, hoping to find her father's black work boots and her little sister's walkers. There are too many black work boots, too many red children's walkers, and no one pair of shoes is distinguishable from the next. All the laces are torn. All the buckles are broken. Soldiers align along the stone pathway as though Esther will walk between them as a dignitary.

At the southwest corner of the crematorium, which looks like the Lincoln Logs cabins my sons built as children, crosshatched strips of serge signify ashes of the German commandant's house torched by Russian troops. Eleven rows of cabbages, thirty-five heads, grow on a knoll in the top quarter of the collage square, above them blue distance and more distant blue clouds drifting up toward the space we understand in art as heaven. The cabbages align with militaristic precision. We call this tactical precision now. At the base of the garden in towering mounds and in the furrows between rows, minute silver-colored stitches depict the cremains shoveled from the furnace of the crematorium, human fertilizer to produce giant cabbage heads. The canisters for the counterfeit ash mementos ostensibly from Buchenwald are outlined in white piping and secured to the fabric back with blanket stitches, the puffy effect of trapunto approximating the ashes stuffed into the canisters. Poles and Ukrainians, during the famine of 1944, washed off the cremains and ate these cabbages.

Susha carried her village recipes in her head. She and Esta Plat learned to roll cabbage leaves together, as young girls working in their mothers' kitchens. During the decades the two friends were apart, my grandmother altered the village recipe for prakas for my mother, who hated raisins in the sauce. The alteration was my grandmother's nod to the new world order. She achieved the sweet-and-sour flavor of the tomato sauce with honey and lemon juice instead of raisins.

Modern recipes just call for ketchup.

History Lesson

I N MAY 1942, NATIONAL SOCIALIST TROOPS WERE garroted in the village of Kortelisy, near Ratne, and partisan Ukrainians and former Red Army soldiers destroyed the local police station then occupied by Nazi troops. Later that summer, still fearing partisan Ukrainian loyalists in the area, retaliations ordered by Heinrich Himmler began for the crime of being Ukrainian and defending Ukrainian land. According to Karel C. Berkhoff in *Harvest of Despair*, the man in charge of the execution of all the town's civilians, Reichskommissariat Kovel' District Commissar Kassner, assembled all the villagers on September 23, 1942, and told them he was going to burn them alive in their homes. After deliberating, he said he'd decided to shoot them instead. A few were spared, but the rest, according to Berkhoff, "were shot with submachine guns, pistols, drowned, or bayonetted to death." Those chosen to live were directed to go to Ratne, because Ratne was deserted. The month before, in August, Ratne's population of more than seven thousand, Jews and non-Jews, had been murdered, with just a handful that escaped under the cover of heavy smoke.

Two teenaged sisters, Marusia and Anastasiia Korneliuk, Ukrainians from Kortelisy, survived the massacre of their townspeople by hiding in a hayloft. Once they emerged, Marusia noticed that those spared from execution were wearing white arm bands, so she tore her white headscarf in two and wrapped the pieces around her arm and her sister's. Berkhoff reports that the girls survived and found their way to relatives in a village near Ratne.

Along the way to Ratne, the girls were approached by the ghost of Esta Plat. At first they were embarrassed by Esta's naked body, but Marusia and Anastasiia had just listened hour by hour to the gunshots killing all the people in their village. They were bruised from where their pounding hearts broke their ribs and ripped open their chests as a blood tide filled their village. So what that Esta's breasts hung unfettered from her shoulder blades. So what that Esta's graying mons was swollen, caked with dirt from her newly shoveled grave. She beckoned to the girls, and with her arms outstretched, urged them closer like a Madonna of the dispossessed. It was then that Anastasiia realized that she would never again feel her mother's or grandmother's breasts pressed against her heart in an embrace. The realization seared her tongue, and when Anastasiia stumbled on the road, Esta went to her and lifted her off the ground as she had done so many times for her children and grandchildren when they were learning how to walk.

Taking care not to step on Esta Plat's arthritic toes, Anastasiia and Marusia pressed themselves against the once-ample flanks of Esta Plat, each sister to a side, then moved together in their hunger and their need as Esta drew them close. Esta's breasts were softer than a winter feather bed, and just as warm. Her legs were warm, her arms! The girls could feel Esta's lifeblood bubbling like the batter for a crepe. They stood and let themselves be transfused, transfixed by the fragrance that arose from the core of Esta Plat, the promise of a distant spring.

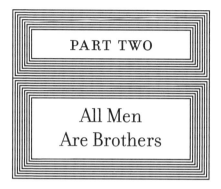

PART TWO

All Men
Are Brothers

Shoahtecture II

R AIN AT THE KZ MEMORIAL CEMETERY OUTSIDE OF Vaihingen an der Enz (Vaihingen-Enz), a perfect, dreary day. The GPS map my husband and I followed placed us at the bottom of a shallow ravine near the bank of the Enz, and we drove back and forth alongside the river's marsh, the cursor on the car's GPS map always pointing into the middle of the river. The swampy mud reminded me of how my mother spoke about the Old Country, if she spoke about it at all: uninhabitable, cold, wet, and filthy and loathsome.

The memorial for Camp Wiesengrund spreads over a few acres that included the camp's refurbished delousing shower house, now a small theater projection space for viewing documentaries including footage of French troops' liberation of the camp in 1945. Another building housed a small exhibition space with historical information, photographs, and teaching materials compiled for local students who visit to learn about their country's history. Nearby, the cemetery interred identifiable bodies that had been reburied from the mass grave for Russian, Polish, Danish, Dutch, French, Romanian, and Hungarian prisoners moved there in 1944 from other camps, also Jews from Radom and Łódź and non-Jewish prisoners of war from camps in Germany—Neckarelz, Trier, Dachau—most of whom succumbed to disease, cold, exhaustion, and starvation in the camp. Over 1,500 typhus-infected men were left in the KZ camp to die without medical treatment, and 280 of these were Jews.

The footprint of the camp proper had been bulldozed in the 1950s, surveyed, leveled, then piled with tons of boulders to raise the level of the valley floor for a new train platform built over the camp just outside Vaihingen-Enz. The train heading north toward Mannheim travels in a tunnel through these boulders, under them the char of barracks halls and watch towers, firepits and the outdoor toilet.

Our guide, Rainer Mayer, showed us photographs of recent defamations and vandalism on the wall surrounding the cemetery—one in 2003 when the main memorial stone at the entrance was spray-painted blue with a swastika and satanic symbols. Some of the gravestones were smashed. In November 2005, shortly before we visited for the first time, a makeshift memorial with candles was arranged in front of the low cemetery wall to commemorate the Munich Beer Hall Putsch of 1928, during which Hitler stormed an industrialists' meeting, starting a riot that landed him a two-year jail sentence, after which his popularity surged.

There were many concentration camps in this region, in addition to the Munich area camp of Dachau. Some members of the Vaihingen-Enz community were opposed to the work Rainer Mayer and other members of the memorial group like our friend Christoph Brudi were doing to establish and preserve this site. *Why dig up the past*, detractors wondered, the phrase a rebuke rather than a question, a challenge to the wearisome notion of *Vergangenheitsbewältigung*, the singular and collective effort to examine the historical past with critical self-reflection.

During World War II, young women from Ukraine had been kidnapped and parceled out to work on German farms like the one owned by the von Neurath family, whose most remote field was seized to construct Camp Wiesengrund. Ten women from Vilika Vovnianka, not too far from Kyiv, were housed in small quarters near the farm's nursery and worked for the von Neurath family until the end of the war, when they were handed over, according to Wendelgard von Staden, to "a commissar from Russia," then controlling Ukraine. They, along with other young Ukrainian women who were forced to work for German families during the war, were exiled at war's end, under Stalin's orders, to labor camps in Siberia, for their so-called crimes of being kidnapped and being forced to work for the enemy. In her memoir, *Darkness Over the Valley*, Wendelgard von Staden (née von Neurath) named some of them—Lida, Sina, Nina, Maruscha.

I fantasized that Esta Plat might have been among these women, still alive, a grandmother, like Susha, many times over, her apron concealing the rotten, fallen apples she'd picked up off the ground as she marched from her small room with the other women through the manor's orchard. She would have appraised the apples' brown and wrinkled skin dotted with black mold, grasped the apples near where the flesh oozed from the split caused by decomposition, tasted the grass and alcohol when she put one to her lips. I thought about the penitent holding the needle-studded apple in Stuttgart during Yom Kippur services, where we'd gone to say the Kaddish after my mother's death, how the man held his apple-mace to his lips, pricking himself until his lips began to bleed.

"They're after us!" a woman said when French troops arrived in Vaihingen-Enz in 1945. "It doesn't matter how old, they're taking all of us." Von Staden crept out of her family's hiding spot late in the night to watch the violence firsthand, for which her long blond hair was shorn by her angry father, as much to protect as punish her.

Soon after, a woman from Vaihingen-Enz fled to the von Neuraths'
manor, asking for their help as thirty soldiers had entered her house
looking for women to rape, soldiers "pushing and shoving on the
staircase" to get upstairs where other women cowered. When the
marauding French soldiers heard Herr von Neurath and their commanding officer enter the house together, they fled down the stairs
past a wall crowded with Bible sayings hanging in glass frames. The
officer escorted the "dazed and bedraggled," half-naked women to
the manor. Addled and terrorized, numb with trauma, the women
nevertheless helped von Staden and her mother cook a meal for
prisoners not yet released from Camp Wiesengrund. Was this the
fate I wished for Esta Plat, just so I could finally say I found her?

Survivors say the best jobs in concentration camps were in the
kitchens, where skimpy rations had their start in pots of mostly
boiling, starchy water. Many of the Jews at Camp Wiesengrund
worked in the kitchen, because some of them had been moved from
Radom, Poland, to Vaihingen-Enz and were free of typhus. This
caused many of the non-Jews, who outnumbered Jews five to one at
the camp, to hate Jews even more.

There were three Dutch survivors of the camp, one a Jew named
Jules Schelvis. During the sixtieth anniversary of the liberation of
the camp in April 2006, Rainer Mayer reported that the two other
Dutch survivors wouldn't speak to Schelvis, who they continued to
believe had received preferential treatment while a prisoner. After
sixty years of freedom, men incarcerated alongside him still bore a
grudge. I imagined *grudge* an ancient word, though it dates around
the years of Martin Luther's life and oozed from envy's tar pit.

Schelvis survived, our guide continued, because he was a master
printer in Amsterdam and the Germans "used his skills," according
to Mayer, to forge documents. He was marched out of Vaihingen-
Enz to Dachau on April 5, 1945, after which he was liberated. He re-

turned to Vaihingen-Enz after the German surrender to work as a nurse for the men with typhus and tuberculosis who were still hospitalized inside the KZ camp.

When we returned from our outing to Camp Wiesengrund, Martin Hartmannsgruber, a former student of mine, came to our flat on Lortzingstraße in Ludwigsburg to practice the English Christmas carols we had agreed to sing with his eighth-grade students in Güglingen. I mouthed such carols when I was a child, as instructed by my mother, conflicted about God and Jesus and anxious about turning into a poisonous toad during requisite participation in Christmas programs that Susha never saw and my mother attended with her eyes closed.

We sang off key in Güglingen, Martin concealing judgment with his signature enigmatic straight-line smile. After our botched C+ performance, students cooked a typical English breakfast with bangers, mash, eggs, toast, and marmite. The food preparation was another kind of cultural endeavor accomplished in the school's home economics lab, especially my team's scrambled eggs. The gooey mess looked like yellow hair balls regurgitated from a cat. We moderated conversation tables with two other American friends, where I learned at my table of teenaged boys that Dennis's favorite song was "Ghetto Gospel" by Tupac Shakur and his uncle owned the largest peanut farm in California. Fine-featured Yannik, blond, blue-eyed, high cheekboned, wanted to join the German military when he got out of school, so that when he came home from future battle, he would be a hero.

Christoph Brudi's retrospective artist's exhibition catalog from 2013, *Figurale Imaginationen*, features an etching composed by Brudi in his summer studio (his barn) in 1986. The haunted image by the haunted son of a war artist is not what young Yannik had in mind when he thought of *hero*. *Hero* to a child has few if any complications, no knowledge of the meaning of all the fields planted with viscera and human teeth to which the hero must attend. What child wants an etching depicting the travail Sad Angel promises the living?

A stooped, nude man pedals west across the etching with his hands, his surreal momentum pent up in his exaggerated, disproportionate body. He is harnessed to a huge wheel like the front wheel of a penny-farthing bicycle. The man's hairline recedes, but his thickly muscled thighs and buttocks are youthful, his face smooth, fine, and lovely as an Etruscan on an urn. In profile, he is focused on his task: perpetually moving forward.

On the man's bent back sits a masked, hooded, caped, or winged figure. I see Sad Angel here, in the nonbinary form suggested by a thin arm, modest bust, fuller head of hair.

One of the angel's arms steadies an enormous mask in front of the man's face. The mask is excessive, heavy, almost as large as the man. The angel looks serious about the task, part of which is to keep the heavy mask from dropping on the ground. The mask is mounted on a pole extended in front of the bent man, and the angel uses the man's back to steady the pole. The man's resignation recalls Sisyphus's travails.

The huge mask in front of the man, like the masks worn by the chorus in Greek drama, suggests the man is engaged in timeless toil and motion, ancient and contemporary. The mask's features are placid, relaxed and closed mouth, beautiful long nose, forward-gazing eyes, lines suggesting thick curls just above the mask's forehead. The world is obscured for the bent man; his eyes don't align with the huge, high, and wide-set eyes on the mask. It is as though he is wearing blinders, like horses being driven in a team.

Sad Angel's forward vision is altered by the mask as well. Whatever is behind the bent man and his driver the two could see, if they chose to look back, or if they could. Looking back would be difficult for both of them; the bent man would need to unyoke himself from the wheel's harness and Sad Angel would need to manipulate the long pole to keep the huge mask aloft. Each of them is stuck in their contorted postures, the man toiling forward, Sad Angel guiding. Where they are going, and why, seems predetermined, or at least orchestrated, into a void of perfect loveliness or dread.

In the Shadow
of the Hotel Silver

EVERY FAMILY HAS A FAVORITE BAKERY. WHEN SU-sha was a girl in Ratne, her mother baked the Shabbat challah. After, when Esta Plat had a family of her own, cottage industries in Ratne sprang up for baking challah, white bread, and occasional cakes like the ones served to welcome former Ratners visiting from their new homes in Buenos Aires, on a mission to encourage everyone to flee Ratne while they could. When Susha lived on Newton Street, she bought bismarks and chocolate-filled eclairs at Mildred's Kosher Grocery on the corner of her street, baked at Frost's, and only Frost Bakery's mother store on West Colfax sold *eier kichlach*, Frost's unsweetened biscuits, like sailor's hardtack, that Susha liked to dunk in her afternoon black coffee.

Harry Grenville's favorite bakery was one in Stuttgart, near the Hotel Silver. Their products were more refined than Frost Bakery's, not confined to worry over kashruth dietary rules. Nineteen thirty-eight was the last time Harry, Heinz Greilsamer then, and his German father, Jakob, satisfied their craving for *Mohrenkopf*, a confection then called Head of the Moor. Jakob had just completed a meeting with a business associate, and before he and his twelve-year-old son, Harry, returned to their home in Ludwigsburg, they speculated about the flavor of this day's treat, chocolate-covered marshmallow crème on a shortbread base, served inside a shop within the long, thin penumbra of the Hotel Silver, the local nickname for the police headquarters occupied by the gestapo in Stuttgart. Who would not be delighted with such a tasty cookie?

Head of the Moor, once also called *Negerkuss* (Negro Kiss), is not flat on top like a fez, not pointed like hamantaschen, not a dunce cap or one half of a fool's cap or shaped like the wizard hats male Jews were forced to wear in Worms in the fourteenth century. Head of the Moor is a nineteenth-century confection, a cornucopia of flavor, a thin shell of chocolate embracing fluffy, whipped egg whites. When corporate bakeries renamed their products to gloss over their racist monikers, the cookie was renamed *Schokokuss* (Chocolate Kiss). Nabisco made them in the United States with the name Mallomars.

The last time Harry and his father stopped at the bakery for their Chocolate Kiss, a new, neatly lettered sign in the right-hand corner of the bakery window that read "No Jews" announced the owner's allegiance to anti-Jewish boycotts. Though Jakob and Harry patronized the shop as all the other customers did, their creeds unknown or unacknowledged, Jakob and Harry turned away from the bakery and returned to Ludwigsburg, menace trumping treat.

Shoahtecture III

SYNAGOGENPLATZ,

LUDWIGSBURG, GERMANY

A BLOCK FROM MATHILDENSTRAßE 8, HARRY GREN-ville's childhood home, photos from the Ludwigsburg archive of Synagogenplatz show the evolution of the Synagogenplatz memorial. At one time, a new bank was proposed to fill the site of the erased synagogue, its foundation to be set inside the old synagogue's footprint, but those plans were ultimately nixed, not entirely because of newfound conscience. By 1988, ten linden trees had been planted for a formal memorial, the play park there replaced with ten water-logged trees, a chiseled granite stone, and a tidy privet hedge.

In 2014, the memorial was reengineered after long committee deliberation on the redesign by Förderverein Synagogenplatz Ludwigsburg, spearheaded by Jochen Faber, the lindens cut, the surface of the park regraded and repaved, new gravel dyed a calming shade of rose. Large, brown facsimile suitcases arranged akimbo recalled the ones that Jews from Ludwigsburg and elsewhere were ordered to pack when they were stripped of their German citizenship and forced to vacate their Ludwigsburg homes en route to processing centers that led to exile and death. The facsimiles were fastened deep into the ground with special bolts and screws to counter tampering, and several clear coats of a varnish were applied, formulated to deflect graffiti or at least make it easier to clean.

Rather than a record of the presence of the worship of God in that spot, noted on an info-stele, the suitcases, with their white, hand-lettered surnames painted on them, including Jakob Greilsamer's, Harry Grenville's father, emphasized in the minds of younger German activists the essential connection all the citizens of Ludwigsburg have with the deportation and murder of some of them. Or at least that's how I explain it to myself, since suitcases to me are large, unwieldly objects that hardly fit into any closet and are impossible to carry without carts or built-in wheels that always break. What meanings or attachments could an etching of a quaint, exotic, mosquelike synagogue convey to people who had never met a Jew except at school assemblies?

The ceremony for the rededication of the memorial for the Ludwigsburg synagogue was held on November 10, 2014. It featured several historians and clergymen; the then mayor of Ludwigsburg, Werner Spec; and Harry Grenville, now a retired biology teacher, ushered with his sister, Hannah, out of Germany and relocated to England during the Kindertransport in 1939.

Harry stood protected from the rain by a heavy white canvas canopy, his trim, slightly stooped frame propped by the podium. The evening was chilly and damp and he wore a winter coat and a small-brimmed loden Alpine hat. Black, thick-framed glasses were snug against the bridge of his small nose, his cheeks flushed by cold, his chin distinct. He addressed the audience in a resolute and crisp voice, describing, in precise and formal German, how Kristallnacht unfolded as witnessed from his home a block away.

First, the sound of shouts. Then, the crackle of flames shooting up the synagogue's walls on Solitudestraße. The flames sounded like cracking walnut shells, Harry said, and the pop of firecrackers. Black soot and smoke shrouded the streets and the apartments all around. Harry described how blistering hot his side of the window felt as he gazed at his once-familiar streets, suddenly foreign, filled with stocky, determined men who moved in their finest official clothing—trilby hats and thick wool coats, baggy high-waisted pants, their bodies floating in and out of blocky focus as they navigated smoke. Other men milled around the edges of the flames with their hands concealed in their pockets, yet others rushed to help uncurl the cloth water hose, aiming the nozzle, carefully, wetting down the walls of buildings and roofs adjacent to the synagogue so that they would remain unharmed. The hiss of steam was louder than a train.

The Harry Grenville I imagined from newspaper photos stood straighter at the podium than this man, his face more angular, his skin tighter. Several images of Harry quickly coalesced, the distinguished guest at the Ludwigsburg ceremony, the bespectacled professor photographed in his Dorchester, England, study surrounded by his books, the pensive citizen in another photo in the *Ludwigsburg Gazette* taken at the conclusion of an interview in 2007, when Harry Grenville asserted that he bore the German people no ill will for murdering his family.

A guest of the Ludwigsburg Stolpersteine Initiative Group, Harry had also been a guest of honor in the city of his birth during the 2009 installation of the *Stolpersteine* blocks memorializing his mother, Klara Greilsamer; his grandmother, Sara Ottenheimer; and his father, Jakob Greilsamer, the three evicted in 1941 from the family home at Mathildenstraße 8 to a crammed multifamily Jew-apartment in Stuttgart, deported to Theresienstadt in August 1942, murdered in Auschwitz on October 28, 1944.

Harry's audience was cloaked in darkness, me among them. A jazz ensemble played a few tunes before the ceremony began, the music, according to event organizer Jochen Faber, meant to soften the edges of the evening's purpose. Harry summarized the history of the family's five-generations roots in the town, beginning in

1870, and concluded on this November evening in 2014 by observing that while frost was trying to coalesce, three generations of the family were present for the rededication—Harry, one of his sons, his grandsons, and nephews, though no one named Greilsamer or Ottenheimer lives in Ludwigsburg now. Harry's voice cracked, his train of thought interrupted. The audience lowered their heads and averted their gaze from the podium, in, what? Shame? Embarrassment for his loss? Embarrassment for his loss of composure? Were they embarrassed to witness his grief? Embarrassed for their grandfathers? No one said.

Harry bent his head and summoned his will to conclude his speech with his dignity in check, summoned his will to focus. He asked the audience to join him in a minute of silent prayer to remember all those lost in the wake of Nazi persecution in Ludwigsburg—Jews, communists, labor organizers, mentally and physically disabled children and adults, Jehovah's Witnesses, Romani. Silence filled every member of the crowd, held fast by their skin.

Harry donned his hat again and cleared his throat. A woman standing next to me with long, wavy silver hair cascading down her back leaned closer to remark quietly. We'd spoken earlier in the afternoon in a dress shop in the central square, where she'd laughed when the young clerk handed her a free-entry coupon to the lady's-night male striptease performance in the Eberhard Wilhelm Shopping Mall, that evening's competing entertainment with the Synagogue Memorial rededication. She'd pointed at the coupon and joked about the stripper's highly erotic bus driver costume.

She smoothed her black leather gloves over the backs of her hands and buttoned her wool tweed coat up to the collar. Before the afternoon I'd seen her with other riders practicing dressage in the arena near the Monrepos villa. Perhaps it was her horse's shit I'd stepped in on the bridal path. Pointing to the facsimile suitcases, she said, "This stings—the suitcases, this man's speech, the stele over there with all the names of the deported from Ludwigsburg."

She shook her head with a gesture I thought meant sad recognition; either that, or she was getting cold. "This is the desired effect."

What is Shoahtecture's desired effect? That evening still plays vivid in my mind, dear Esta, the strains of jazz, people milling in the square stamping their feet and slapping their hands together against the cold, uneasy middle-aged parents with their children gathered tightly around them for a civic history lesson. Mitigated politeness made people look anywhere but at the facsimile suitcases holding imaginary sweaters, imaginary belts and trousers, dresses, toothbrushes, combs, small dolls made from socks. I thought about the musical scores of Czech composer Viktor Ullmann smuggled in a suitcase out of Theresienstadt, his String Quartet no. 3 and Piano Sonata no. 6, his songs from Yiddish folklore and the poems of Friedrich Hölderlin, Hölderlin's "Evening Fantasy" set to music like the spell jazz cast over Harry Grenville's audience, "the golden world" shining "peacefully" until the spell is broken. Is that the desired effect, to see a glimmer of the golden world arising from the ashes?

The deterioration of the former Synagogenplatz memorial's trees and the eroded shortcut scar through the center of the ghost synagogue's architectural footprint made the site a squalid mess. Everybody thought so. Many ideas were presented to remedy the drainage, erosion, and visual problems—stylistic girders, modernist menorahs, incomplete Stars of David like the ones at the Prokhid Hills Memorial outside of Ratne, more information stele like the concrete forest at the Memorial to the Murdered Jews of Europe in Berlin, yet these oversized suitcases placed akimbo resonated with committee members most. A suitcase is not a house of God nor is a holy essence in it, as in the Ark of the Covenant. More important than just the footprint of the synagogue, they agreed by committee vote, was the tangible reduction, haste, and erasure implied by inert suitcases. How was it possible that one suitcase could hold a householder's essential needs, that the suitcase would be identified with a surname painted in regulated letters. Surely the suitcases bolted in gravel in disarray grate against an ingrained preference for symmetry, not to mention that the real owners of the real luggage are so resolutely really dead.

What was the beautiful woman standing next to me at the unveiling thinking? How difficult her own decision would be concerning what to pack? How inhumane this deportation? How unspeakable this murder? How remote this period of the German past? How ghastly? How damnably annoying to chew on it like a ruminant its cud? Were her thoughts pragmatic, along the thoughts of mine—do others here think I am a Jew, and what of that? What of that! Is she feeling paranoia, fear, her amygdala swollen from the size of a tiny almond to a baseball in her brain? Are those tears, or are her eyes watering from wind?

Heirlooms

EINZ GREILSAMER CHOSE THE NAME HARRY GREN-
ville as his nom de guerre in 1944 when he joined the British army, finally of age to serve the adopted country that
had agreed to shelter him. He'd been browsing books in the Jagos'
home library, his British foster family in Cornwall, and a biography
of Vice Admiral Sir Richard Grenville caught his eye. Harry had
wanted to choose a non-German-sounding surname that began
with the letter *G*, the surname change from a Jewish-sounding one
required by the British army, in the event of his capture.

Harry was approaching ninety when we met, and rather than
Mohrenkopf, we spooned cherry vanilla ice cream, one small scoop
each, from crystal dessert cups at an Italian restaurant in Dorchester. I'd been moved by Harry's recollections at the Synagogenplatz
Memorial rededication, so vivid compared to the next to nothing
I knew about Esta Plat and my family around the time of Kristallnacht. With the help of Jochen Faber, journalist and the director of
the Synagogue Memorial reconstruction and the Stolpersteine Initiative projects in Ludwigsburg, I arranged to speak with Harry in
Dorchester.

The Italian restaurant where we lunched caters to retirees who crave the Atlantic sea breeze without the hippy inflection in seaside Brighton. The ice cream isn't rich, chocolate, or butter laced, and the meal itself was not German dumplings or Ludwigsburg's signature spaetzle egg noodles with chanterelles in cream sauce. We dined on potato-leek soup, tagliatelle with Stilton cheese, and cherry vanilla ice cream, every dish the same basic beige with one sprig of parsley in the soup, a dash of fresh-ground pepper on the pasta, and artificially colored cherries scattered through the ice cream, everything served quickly in lumpy blobs so the chef could close the kitchen for the afternoon.

"Who would have thought industrialized murder could go on for so long," Harry said as he hurried a maraschino cherry around his dessert cup with a stainless-steel spoon. "Before he put me on the train to Frankfurt in 1939, my father said he'd see me again, soon. He was so nonchalant. He tried his best to put me at ease, and I believed him."

Harry was framed by a faded yellow-and-green map of Italy behind him, above it a streamer with miniature Italian flags. He ran his hand down the placket of his white shirt, smoothed his blue silk ascot. He must have told this anecdote hundreds of times to many sympathetic listeners, but his hand trembled as he tucked the stray edges of the ascot into his collar, and in the same deadpan with which he pronounced that we would have cherry ice cream to conclude our lunch, he said, "Grandfather often remarked that there must be thousands and thousands of good, decent Germans. 'This will all blow over' was his favorite line." He caught the cherry he was after and raised the spoon to his lips, chewed the lone piece of inoculated fruit like gristle, swallowed with effort.

"Grandfather couldn't have been more deceived." Harry's brow remained unfurrowed, no flush on his sallow cheeks betrayed his sarcasm, a perfect English gentleman, well groomed, well mannered, well dressed, soft-spoken, articulate, undemonstrative.

"I'll show you something," he said, shifting onto one haunch to retrieve a small, tattered card printed with the Kaddish he carries in his back pocket. "My daughter insists we go to the yearly York-minister Anglican Evensong service on December 15. I take this card and read the Kaddish under my breath for my parents, grand-mother, and Aunt Hilde while they're singing."

As he spoke, the few other patrons in the restaurant conversed loudly about the recent shootings at the *Charlie Hebdo* office and the Paris kosher supermarket nearby. "I heard a woman say she was going to take her family out of France," a diner said, placing her menu on the table.

"Jews are never happy anywhere," another said.

Harry pushed his glasses up his nose and made an offhanded wave over the crown of his head. "See. Everyone is an expert about what Jews think," he said. "Everyone knows what Jews should do."

Jews should forgive. That is what Jews should do.

Though I had a list of questions to ask Harry during our afternoon visit, he guided the conversation with his own remarks. When we arrived at his flat, his dining room table was covered with books he'd pulled from his library shelves about Ludwigsburg, as though he were the head of the local chamber of commerce. His most prized, *Ludwigsburg und das Land*, a *Heimatbuch*, is a chronicle of local studies concerning Ludwigsburg and environs, written in the Swabian dialect, Harry's mother tongue. The book had been gifted to every school-age child in Ludwigsburg before the Nuremberg Laws forced Harry to attend the Jews-only school in Stuttgart. The gift made Harry feel like one of the guys.

I leafed through photographs of requisite landmarks, the Ludwigsburg Palace, the Napoleonic gates to the city on Schorndorfer Straße, constructed to prevent soldiers garrisoned in Ludwigsburg from sneaking away, close to what is now the Central Office of the State Justice Administrations for the Investigation of National Socialist Crimes.

"I miss the sounds of Swabian," Harry said. "Not many people speak it anymore. To many it sounds uneducated, so we use standard German now." I wanted to say something comparative about Yiddish, but I already knew what Germans think of Yiddish. When Susha was learning English in Denver as a young woman, a German-Jewish woman had described the Yiddish that newer immigrants spoke as a medley performed courtesy of some of the body's sphincters—farting, belching, and expectorating phlegm.

Harry described playing as a boy at the edges of the pond in the brickyard north of the Ludwigsburg main train station, scooping and channeling sand to build dams, catching salamanders and trapping frogs, fishing in Monrepos Lake. In his excitement to commandeer a rowboat, he once broke an oar on a metal pipe that spewed water into the man-made lake.

As he described the pile of sooty bricks delivered to the brickyard after Kristallnacht and the demolition of the synagogue, Harry's voice tightened. He picked out a book with a black cover and a plastic spiral-bound spine. "Aunt Hilde made this for my mother," Harry said, patting the cover. "She collected the letters and photographs my mother sent her while Hannah and I were growing up, excerpted the letters and shared the photographs so my mother would have a memento of us while we were in England.

"We were all certain we would be reunited after the war," he said again.

Backgrounded by young, leafed-out maples, Jakob Greilsamer stands in one photograph behind Harry and Hannah in the park surrounding the Ludwigsburg Palace. Jakob wears a three-piece suit, stiff white collar, tightly knotted diagonal-striped tie with a tie clip, an Alpine hat tight and even across his forehead like Harry had worn to the Synagogue Memorial rededication in Ludwigsburg. The hat brim shadows Jakob's brow, and though unsmiling, Jakob seems proud and pleased, fit and capable, a man then in his early sixties raising his young family. His hand rests lightly on young Harry's shoulder, Harry in lederhosen with a short-sleeved white button-down shirt, his sister, Hannah, next to him in a sleeveless empire-waist dress with a white Peter Pan collar. The dress has one pocket close to the hem, and the sharp corner of a pressed handkerchief pokes above the rim. Hannah's face is blurred in the photo, suggesting that she wiggled, turned her head, or sneezed, but Harry wears a sharp and happy air of nonchalance, his left hand concealed inside his deep pocket, perhaps clutching a stone or a small frog he scooped up from the fountain in the Ludwigsburg Palace courtyard. He poses willingly, patiently, as his mother captures her adoration on film.

Hilde Ottenheimer had begun this keepsake book for her sister, Klara, while she was teaching at a Jewish high school in Berlin, having been barred, after receiving her doctorate in criminology in 1934, from teaching at Friedrich Wilhelm University, also in Berlin.

"If only Aunt Hilde had taken more care," Harry said suddenly, breaking the silence, pique sliding underneath the barrier of his manners. "The letters should not have been excerpted; they should have been recorded in their entirety." He tapped his fingertips lightly on the table and adjusted the volume of the hearing aids tucked behind his ears. "Then, there would have been a record of anti-Semitism and how it affected the family in the day to day. It was so . . . pervasive. So mundane."

I leafed quickly through the compendium, a memento of photographs and prose recreating the bonds of the family. The album's gaze and voice are Klara's, reinforcing the fragile joy and love she and Jakob had for their children.

"Are you sure your mother would have confided in her sister," I said.

"Absolutely," Harry said. "I heard my parents talking at night when they thought we were asleep."

With the perfect hindsight no one except Sad Angel has, Hilde Ottenheimer might have known that despite her scholarship on Jews in German culture, her work with Leo Baeck and her editing of *Germania Judaica*, she would be deported on October 19, 1942, transported by train to Riga, Latvia, where a mob of pitchfork-wielding convicts often met these Jew-trains. She was murdered in the Riga ghetto two days later.

"At least you have this," I said. I traced the white rectangular paper glued to the cover that held the book's title as though it were the Aleppo Codex rather than this family scrapbook with a plastic spine. "The only record we had of our family in Ukraine was a bundle of letters that was lost."

Harry looked out the window as he ran his fingertips across the edge of his silk ascot. The African violets on the sill were about to blossom purple. He reached out as if to caress one of the soft green petals on a plant then trained his gaze on me. Eyes that had sparkled during lunch turned dull and cold. For a split second, it occurred to me he could be having a stroke. How many scores of responses like mine deflated his unique and profound grief, responses that compromised his luck, information that tipped the perfect balance in a moral universe where one story is the best story, where one photograph is the emblematic photograph.

"Ukraine," he finally said, as though the word smelled like soot like soil like scorn. "Pity."

The late afternoon filled then with tangible regret. A plate of chocolate-covered cookies sat untouched on the table. Harry took a phone call from his son, said he felt quite well, asked about his son's heart, and promised to call him back as soon as I was gone. He checked his wristwatch and the clock on the wall above the phone. Fatigue seemed to wash over him, weary after yet another afternoon wading through a lifetime of progress and regret.

Harry Grenville dwelled in several concurrent realities, judging from the books in his library, the histories of World War II, the complete works of Adorno, Levi, Arendt, Wiesel, the poems of Paul Celan and Nelly Sachs, in front of a few of the books a framed photograph of him and his wife, Helen, at a Shinto shrine in Japan taken during one of their last trips together. His imagination was defined, he confided during the afternoon we spent together, by three journeys: the first from Ludwigsburg to Frankfurt to Holland to Cornwall during the Kindertransport; the second the journey he imagined in a never-ending nightmare—his father, mother, and grandmother deported from Germany to Theresienstadt to their deaths in Auschwitz; and the third, the journey Harry took in 2009 via the Eurostar and TGV high-speed trains to the *Stolpersteine* ceremony to commemorate his family's five-generations rootedness in Ludwigsburg, his claim to place. The brass plaques on the faces of the *Stolpersteine* cemented into the sidewalk outside the family's former home on Mathildenstraße 8 for Harry's father, mother, and grandmother are what remain of the intimate record of Harry's childhood home, small commemorative wafers of etched copper over stone polished up by local volunteers, dulled again by footsteps, baby carriage wheels, and rain.

In a letter dated April 1945, posted in Switzerland, Bella Schmal wrote to a relative in Basel about the fate of Jakob and Klara Greilsamer and Sara Ottenheimer. Schmal had been a prisoner in Theresienstadt as well, released to "finish up," Harry said, in Switzerland in 1945, and by that I took Harry to mean finish up her incarceration as a stateless person. In the corner of her letter, "in terrible handwriting," Harry noted, she recounted how Klara's name alone had been added to the list of other prisoners in Theresienstadt ordered to assemble in October 1944 for relocation in the east, which everyone knew meant Auschwitz. When they learned the news, unwilling to let Klara make that journey alone, Jakob and Sara volunteered to go along with Klara. All three were murdered in Auschwitz when they arrived.

I understood Harry's anecdote in several ways. I think it was a comfort to him to know that his parents and grandmother were with one another during their transport to Auschwitz, and that at least mother and daughter were close to each other when they died, or at least that's the thought. Jakob Greilsamer and Sara Ottenheimer seemed heroic, sacrificing themselves in order to provide whatever comfort they could to Klara.

Shlomo Venezia, a survivor of a *Sonderkommando* unit in the gas chambers of Auschwitz, described in *Inside the Gas Chambers* what death from Zyklon B gas looked like, how when the chambers were opened after the gas had been released, Venezia and his unit took out clumps of corpses and moved them to the crematoria. It was evident that prisoners clawed and bit and battered one another, climbed on top of one another's heads and shoulders to get above the shower heads. Harry had access to this information, but that kind of torment he kept deep within himself.

A decade after Harry Grenville married Helen Westmacott in Cornwall, he received a letter from his sister, Hannah, who had married a Sinologist from the American Midwest. Hannah and her husband attended a Sinology conference in Cologne in the mid-1950s, and they stopped in Ludwigsburg to see if they could find the S—s, neighbors of the Greilsamers before the Greilsamers were evicted from their home and forced to move to Stuttgart. Klara had entrusted her sister Hilde's album of photographs and excerpted letters to their neighbors for safekeeping in their store on the corner of Mathildenstraße.

The S—s, a childless couple, returned the album during a strained afternoon of tea and Chocolate Kisses in their home, served perhaps on the Greilsamers' heirloom silver. Before Hannah and her husband departed, Mrs. S— asked Hannah and her husband if they wanted to buy the silver back. Klara had bartered it piece by piece for food during the hiatus between generalized rationing and food purchases allocated to Jewish families in designated groceries where Jews were permitted to shop. During the gap, as Harry recounted, there was no food for Jews in Ludwigsburg except through barter.

How much food would a silver cake knife buy, or a fork, a scalloped jam spoon, a cream pitcher, or a vessel for sugar? A sack of flour, or just a few tins of processed meat scraps laced with lard? A half-kilo of dried beans? A quarter kilo of powdered milk? How many apples would a tea pot bring? And the broad serving tray with braided silver handles, how many cone-head cabbages and potatoes? Heads of the Moor, called by any name, atop a white paper doily, would look elegant arrayed on the Greilsamers' silver tray.

Harry and Hannah had already made their journey to England when food rationing and extortion began in Ludwigsburg. They had no direct memory of their mother's bartering except in redacted postcards from their parents forwarded to England by the German Red Cross. The deprivation of their family members continues to wound. Perhaps the S—s never intended to give the silver back, thus the exorbitant price they asked; perhaps the German couple had made no inquiries about the fates of their neighbors, the Greilsamer and Ottenheimer families, and so were shocked when Hannah contacted them. Perhaps the price the S—s asked for the entire service indicated their dire straits. Perhaps, like the liberated prisoners from the KZ Camp in Vaihingen-Enz, Harry and Hannah had no emotional capacity to assuage the S—s, regardless of the couple's motivations. Perhaps Harry and Hannah wished to sever the tacit responsibilities of one family to the other, if that is ever possible. Perhaps they wanted to be done with the Holocaust.

When Harry collaborated with the Ludwigsburg *Stolpersteine* group to write the narrative for his parents' and grandmother's memorial ceremony before their *Stolpersteine* were cemented into the sidewalk in front of the family's last residence in Ludwigsburg, Harry asked one of the group members, Gudrun Karstedt, to help him look for the S—s or learn when and where they died. Harry didn't say what he might have done if Karstedt had found the couple. He merely told me he was satisfying "a curiosity."

It is no small feat for Germans to disappear without a record or a trace, but the S—s did.

And yet. Because the S—s kept and returned Aunt Hilde's scrapbook, a physical record of Harry's childhood and his childhood home remain intact, now in multiple copies. For Harry's children and their families, there is evidence of Harry's parents, grandparents, beloved aunt, the early life they shared together in Ludwigsburg, an idyllic place Harry Grenville still calls home.

Blue Moon

CHEŁMITES, THE CITIZENS OF MYTHIC POLISH Chełm, bore the brunt of many Yiddish jokes. Simpletons and fools, Chełmites were challenged by the dark, no matter stars, and on the darkest nights, when they ventured out along their rutted roads, they stepped in dung or fell or tripped and broke their arms and legs. Chełmites couldn't add though they followed the Kabbalah, and the universe they inhabited was not graced by the Haskalah, wherever that enlightenment might be.

Chełmites knew nothing of the world but Chełm, and even then, their knowledge was limited to the observation of their goats and breadcrumbs in their rebbes' beards. Though eastern Europeans told jokes about Polish Chełm, even if they, too, were from eastern Europe, Chełmites endured the cruelties hurled at those who happened to be born in shanty settlements on the borders of the Pale. If Mrs. Schwartz on Newton Street in Denver forgot to trim her mustache before she went to Mildred's Kosher Grocery for a slice of halvah, she was certainly from Chełm, and if a man rolled down his car window and hocked a loogie on West Colfax Avenue,

Chełm was written on his license plate forever after. Bubbies who survived the camps and took all the sugar packets, grape jelly, and little plastic thimbles full of cream from the silver dispensers at the Village Inn Pancake House, people winked and blamed the bubbies' parsimony on their former citizenship in Chełm.

People said when Chełmites talked it sounded like bleating goats, and when they farted the stench lingered like the odor of decomposing cows farmers threw on the edges of their cornfields. If a cousin just off the boat misconjugated verbs, said "ain't" or jumbled cases, what could you do but cringe about a Chełmmite who had grown up in a rough-hewn log house with a thatch roof no one would park their car in now. So ingrained was the wish to transcend Chełm that many families, like mine, changed their surnames to German-Jewish ones.

One day, a Chełmite overheard a man from Vilnius boasting that Vilnius was so great the night sky above the city was illuminated like candles blazing in a chandelier. "*Nu?*" the man said to no one in particular, "why should Chełm be any different?"

He devised a plan.

The Chełmite waited for the Blue Moon night, the fullest summer moon, in Elul (August). Stealthily, he approached his water barrel, board in one hand, hammer in the other, nails lined up all along his lips, with the rusty-tasting heads resting on his tongue. The luminous moon in the water barrel pained the man and almost blinded him, just as touching fire will sear and blister flesh. The light was mesmerizing; it took all the man's will to wrench his gaze away. When he looked at the rim of the barrel, then at the rainspout coming off the roof, and farther afield, at his neighbor Favel's broken wagon wheels and the open door of Favel's privy, he saw haloes of rainbow colors everywhere, dancing pinwheels, the blues, indigos, and violets at the end of the rainbow's spectrum. Back and forth, he gazed and looked away, until there were circles of color

dancing up and down the dusty streets of Chełm, in the alleys, on
the rooftops, on the synagogue door, the chimney of the town's
bake oven, even on the dot of his donkey's anus.

When the moon's illumination filled his chest, all four chambers of his heart, his stomach, his throat, his intestines, bowels, the
little white quarter moons at the very bottom of his fingernails, he
stepped fully into the moon's light. There he saw the shadow of the
tall, straight-backed, long-legged, and hard-cocked fellow who had
been, until that moment, hiding deep within his crippled, hunch-
backed body. He saluted his better brother, placed the board over
the water barrel's mouth, and nailed it down.

And then, the man waited. While he waited, he harvested a cabbage and his wife made him prakas, just the way he liked them, with
honey she bought from Esta Plat's famous Ratne hives. He waited
until a night overcast with clouds, no moon, no stars, nothing but
the anemic flicker of candles in the windows of the rickety houses
of Chełm. It was so dark he stepped on his sleeping donkey's tail
as he groped his way along the edge of his house to the rain barrel, clasping a crowbar in both hands. The bray of the injured beast
jabbed the silence and made the man's heart race, but the man held
tight to the crowbar as he slipped the smooth, beveled end between
the board and the rim of the barrel and levered the bar until the
nails gave way.

While he worked, the man thought about how beautiful his beloved had been by the light of the full Blue Moon, how so many
years before, its light on her breasts made them smooth and cool,
how the dimples in her nipples had winked at him, and how, nine
months later, moonlight bathed the brow of their newborn son as
the infant lay between them on their pallet stuffed with straw.

The man closed his eyes so as not to experience the kind of pain
in his skull he'd had when he gazed in the water barrel that other
Blue Moon night. When he opened his eyes and peered into the
pitch-black barrel, at first he thought he'd been struck blind. He

held out his hand in front of his face and saw his wiggling fingers. He closed his eyes again, lowered his head, opened his eyes, again the darkness in the barrel, again his wiggling fingers. Someone had stolen the moon from him! But who could he accuse? Satan? The tsar? Schlomo, the shiftless trickster who tried to tell him to pack his things and run away? Already labeled That Man from Chełm, who would believe him, anyway?

The spirit of the man from Chełm plunged into a deep and profound terror, the kind of terror the rabbis warned of in a godless world.

During a trip to search through holdings from Ukraine at the Wiener Holocaust Library and at the British Library, I went to a concert in the Royal Festival Hall with my son and son-in-law. The London Philharmonic Orchestra played Debussy's *Le Martyre de saint Sébastien* and several other standards. Crossing the bridge over the Thames going back into central London, the moon was in the first quarter. The Thames was inky and turbulent and the waves seemed dangerous and forbidding. When we'd crossed the bridge going over to the south bank earlier in the evening, there'd been a street musician playing the violin. As she played, a group of tourists stopped and rifled in their pockets for change to toss into her violin case, for which she slightly cocked her head in thanks and kept on playing. She'd long since packed up and moved off the bridge, and the river, witness to thousands of generosities and despairs, gave up none of them.

As we stood in the center of the bridge, the Parliament clock tower was softly illuminated, the Parliament building, Westminster Abbey, the red lights along the periphery of the Ferris wheel Eye. Orion's Belt was vivid, as was Aldebaran. A cold wind began to blow, and though we were in the center of the city, the spot was dark, perfect in its privilege of momentary solitude. During our walk back to their flat, there was a quality of light that you wouldn't expect from a city—muted, soft—Trafalgar's statue barely visible atop his pedestal in Trafalgar Square.

I've never been in a dark so complete that I couldn't see my hand in front of my face, not even in the closet of my third-grade classroom, where each of us was ushered by the school nurse, who shone a fluorescent light on our scalps to check for head lice. On a perfect, moonlit, Rocky Mountain night, you can read the pages of a book, see the moons in the cuticles of your newborn son, the saliva on the tongue of the family dog. If Susha had been picking wild blueberries in the forest near Ratne with Esta Plat, she'd be able to see the blue-purple berry stain on Esta's teeth and tongue on Elul's moonlit night.

The Hours of Exile

BEHIND THE LUDWIGSBURG PALACE, AN INFORMA-tion board adjacent to a tree trunk identifies the tree's growth rings with corresponding historical events, the ca-pitulation of Ludwigsburg to Napoleon, the years 1939 to 1945 blank. The tree's deep roots comingled with primal mud, fanned out to drink the waters of the Neckar River before its wetlands were drained to form the palace grounds. Even such a mighty old tree, evidenced by the massive girth of its trunk, had died, had been cut down, chopped up, its residue burned, the ashes mixed into the soil of the baroque-themed gardens on the palace grounds.

Across the street from the palace, in Favoritepark, I had seen a man about my husband's age kissing his wife and smoothing down her disheveled, curly hair, which made me miss my husband in-tensely. He was home, teaching, while I was in Ludwigsburg, teach-ing. I think of him as my place, regardless of our location, and with-out him in Ludwigsburg, I moved through three-dimensional space as though it were two, flat and ungraspable.

The man was stockier than my husband, fuller in the hips and thighs, dressed in a cream-colored button-down shirt, gray slacks worn without a belt, and black wingtips like my husband would never wear. The way the man bent his neck and angled his head to press his lips against hers made me feel the absence of my husband's kiss. The couple stood near the French doors of King Ludwig's hunting palace at the south end of Favoritepark, the colors of its pink stucco and gold leaf filigree window grilles reflecting the morning sun.

Yellow leaves blew around the couples' feet in a miniature tornado. She removed her wrists from her black crutch cuffs to return his embrace, leaned both crutches against the glass panes in the French doors, and rocked forward against his body to balance hers. She must have trusted his rooted stance, because she swayed without hesitation or speaking to him, as though they had practiced this embrace hundreds of times. He didn't reach out his arms to steady her or guide her as she pressed her weight against his core, he just stood, ready to catch her with the strength in his torso.

Once her chest was pressed against his and her face was nuzzled into the hollow of his throat, he embraced her with the tenderness one saves for children. She responded in kind then pushed away, slowly slipping out of her flats. She inched her bare feet onto the man's shoes so that the two could move in unison, a few slow steps, perhaps part of a convalescence regime they had created long ago. Unlike the embrace, the movement of their feet together seemed to cause her pain—her knees locked, her hips stiffened.

Neither the man nor the woman spoke. When she slid off his feet, she slowly curled her toes as though clinging to a ledge before she inched her feet back into her shoes and opened a small gap between their bodies. They smiled shyly at one another, unaware that I had seen them. I felt embarrassed of my curiosity, voyeuristic, envious of their regard for one another, but also trapped in a loop of doubt wondering if my husband would have the patience, or I the humility, to help my convalescence were I to lose the capacity to walk unaided.

I danced in stockinged feet on the tops of my mother's feet in the basement of our house on Winona Court in Denver, keeping time to the motor of the sump pump in the utility room behind us. I loved this embrace, but she did not, nor did she love the pressure of my feet on her metatarsals, which even at her young age then were riddled with arthritis. It was one of the few times we touched during something that resembled play. Little did I know that the one or two times we glided in unison across the polished linoleum floor would end almost as soon as they began. She bought me a life-sized doll to take her place, one with an ugly, oval mouth and rounded blue-cloth feet, thick elastic bands attached to the doll's soles my feet slipped into. The doll was rough, and its stuffing reminded me of the bean bags made from scraps of Art Deco curtains Susha had stuffed with locust pod seeds during Sukkot years before. The doll smelled like dry straw and maple leaves, and my mother seemed disappointed that I did not cherish it.

Before dawn the next morning, I was awakened in my apartment by the low rumble of a semitruck curving through the roundabout at the dead end of Reuteallee. The length of that part of the street between the roundabout and the entrance and exit ramps to the Favoritepark train platform had become an unofficial parking area for long-haul truckers stopped to catch a few hours of sleep, and though I knew this, the low tenor of slowing truck gears unnerved me. Cold, I moved to press against my husband's back but found only the artificial lemon smell of industrial laundry powder and the clammy dampness that had seeped in between the broken slats of silver venetian blinds trying to cover the windows.

The next afternoon I returned to Favoritepark hoping to photograph the mushrooms and fungi I had seen on my morning walk the day before. They weren't the edible *Steinpilz*, wild boletus of the sort Esta Plat harvested, dried, and exported to Susha, *podgrzybek*, but they were beautiful in the way poisonous plants seduce.

Mushrooms absorb the terroir of home, which makes wild

mushrooms precious. Burdock, birch, pines, buck brush, blackberry canes flavor fungal colonies. Hot pink calypso orchids blossom among them in the Rocky Mountain West. Polish boletes renowned for their flavor share the same genus my family hunted when we lived in northeastern Oregon, though after the eruption of Mount Saint Helens in 1980, mushrooms took on the flavor of the volcano's ash.

The terroir surrounding Ludwigsburg carries overtones of slug. Beyond Favoritepark, fields sloping down to the Neckar's banks are brown as chestnuts, darkened by manure and grayed with clay. Manure piles mixed with hay from the horse stables in Monrepos perfume the mud, along with rotting leaves, banana slugs, worms, and standing water. The decomposing material would make some mushrooms swell, but the fields are tilled almost to the edges of the asphalt paths, disturbing everything that might have grown wild there, especially near the lane going down the hill toward Seeschloss, a baroque-style villa in Monrepos.

My husband is usually the record keeper of our collective mushroom-siting gaze, snapping joyous shots of the first morels of the season, the nut-brown lion's mane mushrooms cascading from a rotted log along the trail where we pick chanterelles at the beginning of autumn, the red-and-white-speckled death angels that bloom in the fall in the Elkhorn Mountains, the slippery jacks that erupt just before first snow, never wise to eat. I hadn't been carrying my camera in the morning, as I usually don't, but I thought because it was unseasonably warm, I needed to return at once. If I waited too long, the mushrooms I had seen would get rooted up by the small axis deer herd that roams freely through the park, or deliquesce into a slimy black blob.

Favoritepark is a public park and forested preserve that was once Duke Eberhard Ludwig's hunting park, then that of King Frederick I, then owned by the various dukes of Württemberg. Grouse, pheasant, hares, squirrels, and herds of small hoofed, horned, and antlered mammals roam there. The grounds are separated from the Schloss Ludwigsburg (Ludwigsburg Palace), by Neckarstraße, a four-lane highway that connects motorists with Stuttgart and Frankfurt. Though the three-story hunting lodge is within easy walking distance of the main palace, story has it that when Eberhard Ludwig fancied a few days of concentrated bird and mammal slaughter in his park, it took close to a month to move his entourage out of the palace and across the street, and back.

Irrationally, I think of Favoritepark when I am in Ludwigsburg as my park. I've walked along every pathway in the park, deep into the thin margins of manicured woods, outside the park on asphalt paths that crisscross the countryside that borders Ludwigsburg. Its predictable monotony was compromised only once, when an axis buck charged, antlers menacing, making a beeline toward a doe in estrus that I happened to be standing near.

The park was close to my apartment, and the park grounds are adjacent to the Ludwigsburg University of Education. It is nothing if not genteel, even when a fleet of SUVs arrives with preschool children ready to engage with nature by hitting trees with sticks then sitting on a log to eat their lunch. Its opening and closing hours aligned with the light of each season, which seemed decent and sensible. People greeted one another with furtive glances without breaking their stride.

Aside from the lovers embracing against the backdrop of pink stucco and gold-leaf window grilles, I had never seen other people touching in the park. Over time, I became possessive of the animals trapped there, disturbed when I heard gunshots in the predawn hours as groundskeepers culled the herds. When I spotted soggy wads of frosted sweet rolls left on a stump for deer to nibble and lick, I felt irate about visitors feeding animals processed human food and often brushed the crumbs to the ground, though that did nothing except leave a trail of crusty frosting in the weeds. It was only later, when the grounds crew cut to the quick the tall, thick brambles that formed the living fence around the yard behind my apartment that I asked myself why I pretended intimacy with a stretch of road through a park on a continent my family fled.

Other tourists in Favoritepark out for their own familiar ambles photograph the red squirrels eating bits of buttered pretzels, and the record, over time, of the vegetation that blooms and fades, grasses both browsed and mowed, vines cut back to the ground, trees felled and left to rot and regenerate the tired loam, herds culled—seeing these familiar sights year after year when I arrive to teach makes me feel that I belong, but to what tableau? My ancestors were likely exiled from Germany before Luther's ink was dry. Yet, regardless of the scores of times I have walked in Favoritepark, when I'm not walking there I have felt nostalgia for the lovers in my park and wince recalling the pop of rifle fire signifying the removal of lame, sick, or old animals from my zoo. Why did I insist on personalizing the park in my imagination? I don't call any of the pools where I swim my pools, the lap lane I stake out my lane, any more than I call the grocery cart with the sticking front wheels at the Rewe where I buy my groceries in Ludwigsburg my cart. The Katz Bakery near the Ludwigsburg main train station where I buy spinach quiche and custard tarts? It's my bakery only in my mind. And the greengrocer's stand in Eglosheim where I buy strawberries, plums, and Turkish dates? None of these places are mine. Recognition and habit do not equal possession, let alone the supposed protections citizenship affords. Is this insistence just, as Aristotle suggested, a crutch to stimulate recollection for a moment of tranquility I never really had?

Before a visit to the Stadionbad pool, having walked in the drizzle through Favoritepark and alongside the ambulance entrance to the Klinikum Hospital, I saw a yellow ambulance with its back door open parked away from the portico, where all the waiting ambulances idle, and where patients are unloaded. Inside the opened ambulance door, a dead man was strapped to a gurney, his mouth agape in the *O* of rigor mortis, his face ashen. A small bandage across the bridge of his nose had come unstuck and drooped above his nostril. His steel-colored hair was disheveled. He didn't look old, just dead. One of the ambulance attendants was gathering up a bag with the man's last effects. The attendant wadded the bag as though it were going to be discarded. A blue strap fastened underneath the gurney was cinched around the deceased man's waist to keep him from slipping off while the ambulance was moving.

I have seen only one other corpse, my mother's, so my view of the man was shocking, jarring, intimate. Had I arrived at a moment of belonging? I had a view of the man that his family members didn't, and wouldn't. As I stood watching the attendants pack up the man's things, I felt like an intruder. I hadn't shared anything with the dead man in life, not a slice of a special rhubarb and rum cake at his sixtieth birthday celebration, nor a glass of bubbly *Sekt* at his retirement party, not as a witness to his youngest grandson's baptism or his wife's tears at their only daughter's wedding. We didn't share a creed, or a culture, or a language. Unlike the feeling of watching the woman on crutches, the stab of her husband's kiss reminding me of my husband's absent kisses, my heart didn't clutch over the family's loss for this dead man. I'd never seen him eating cured olives at the Trattoria Rosa Blu on Eberhardstraße, or tearing injera with his fingers at the Ethiopian restaurant near the Torture Museum on Schorndorfer Straße, nor eating a buttered pretzel at the farmer's market in Ludwigsburg's main square. I'd never seen him sipping from a mug of hot glühwein at the Weihnachts fair in early December. I do not share in the depth of the man's family's grief, yet spotting the opened ambulance door made me want to peer inside, dabble with intimacy, just as I wanted to peer in dusk-stained rooms decades ago when I was a student walking across town on my way to the library to study in the evening, to learn how people build their lives around one another in a place they identify as home.

––––––––––

An elderly couple walking inside the gate of Favoritepark just a few steps behind me watched as I crouched to examine a mushroom's pileus and stipe. Though amblers in the park always maintain distance between themselves and unfamiliar others, the woman caught up with me and asked, unbidden, if my hair color was natural. I said yes, and she said very beautiful, and I said thank you. I walked on, irritated by her close proximity and her question, continued snapping random, out of focus photographs of desiccated cream- and ivory-colored fungi, orange rimmed and frilly, some with spiked edges, brown roll rims. At a fork in the main path, where one path continues straight toward the royal hunting lodge and the Ludwigsburg Palace, and the other veers east to an exit from the park into a cultivated rye field, I crouched again to photograph a cluster of orange-golden trumpets, determined to record their similarity to chanterelles, their orange like autumn maples, their cheerful bell-shaped pileus. The woman bent down next to me and put her Nivea-greased cheek against my cheek. "Are you interested in mushrooms?" she asked. I nodded and stood quickly, wanting to run away.

"Oh, my," she said, switching to English, placing her knees on the ground to balance. She turned her neck stiffly to look up at me and fussed with the green chiffon scarf she'd tied around her throat.

"Well, then. I see. What is your language?" She tapped on the cap of one of the mushrooms I had just photographed, and the cap split in two. "Oh," she said again as she stood, "I spoiled your little picture."

"English is my native language," I said, in English.

The woman's husband veered off the walking path to stand beside us. She looked to be in her early eighties, but her husband looked a decade older, my father's age if he had lived a longer life. The man clomped with the help of his black cane, stepping with his right foot, dragging his left until his shoulder touched my shoulder. The dirt dug up by his injured foot defined a low ridge and trough like an unplanted furrow.

"She is interested in mushrooms," the woman said, smoothing the gaps in the buttons on his beige cardigan, speaking loudly into his left ear.

The man studied the impression his dragging foot had made, then looked up to study my face. "You're not from here!" the man shouted, his sudden agitation heightened by his imbalance after he dropped his cane.

"You're Russian!" He leaned into a tree and pounded his small, liver-spotted hand on the rough bark, his pats muted by the layer of insect frass under the bark loosened by his hand. His nails were so immaculate they seemed like translucent pearls glued to the raw tips of his fingers.

"Dear!" the lady shouted to her husband. "You can see she is a ginger! A gin-ger! Gingers live in England and speak English."

"She's a Russian," her husband stammered. "Aren't you?" he said in Russian, pointing at my forehead, my eyes, my chin.

"My husband is from Berlin," the woman said, crossing her right arm across her chest as though about to place her hand over her heart. "Long ago, he was very brave. A hero. Do you know Berlin? Berlin! It is our treasure!" The woman stooped to pick up her husband's cane and hooked the crook over his wrist. From wartime photos, my mother's gaze on her handsome soldier husband said she, too, thought him very brave. Or at least that was the impression in the photos.

The woman had regained her composure and lightly patted the lapel of her camel's hair coat. She paused, and for a moment I thought she was going to apologize for her husband's outburst, but she didn't. "I am from here," she said. "This is our park. It makes us feel proud. We are proud people. We love our animals. We are glad you find our mushrooms interesting, though these particular ones are poisonous to humans, regardless of what the field guides say."

"Your park is lovely," I said, spotting another cluster of dark orange-golden trumpets I wanted to photograph. "I have often felt a sense of calm walking here." I lifted the camera strap over my head. Cradling the camera under my arm, I turned to walk away.

The woman's husband brushed his fingertips across his upper lip, as though he'd forgotten he'd shaved his mustache decades ago. "I can always spot a Russian," he said, shaking his finger.

His wife grabbed him by his left elbow to worry his inert body along, gradually guided him to the forking path leading to the park exit closest to the rye field. A breeze blew dried oak and maple leaves across the path as the couple receded, wending their way out of their park. It was difficult to imagine such an addled old man firing a *Panzerschreck*, looking with patriotic satisfaction at a sea of indistinguishable tanks reduced to nothing.

When the couple reached the gate near the tall, latticed fence at the edge of the park, the man paused and looked back. He dropped his cane, and his wife quickly picked it up and closed his hand around the crook. She put her hand gently on his shoulder and urged him through the turnstile.

Three plosives, "pu, pu, pu," followed my grandmother's shouts of "*Keinehora*!" You! Satan! Step back! And if you don't, I'll spit in both your bloodshot eyes.

In polite company, the voiced *p* "pu, pu, pu" became a mime of expectoration, the full performance the time-honored shtetl ritual to mitigate the power of meddling demons, a mostly futile gesture to deflect the evil eye. Entrenched in Schadenfreude's tenuous bond to retribution, superstitious fear of humans wielding the evil eye while doling superficial compliments, "*Keinehora*!" worms its way into generational memories of hiding from mob and torch. How powerful that word, *keinehora*, roadblock to disaster. *Keinehora*, the terror in my heart. How debilitating, the belief that even in the calm and stasis of photographing mushrooms, one crawls on all fours beneath the hairy balls of tragedy and death. *Keinehora*.

"Apotropaic practices," Michael Wex reminds in his study of the Yiddish language, *Born to Kvetch*, includes sayings, talismans, and deeds, like buying Esta Plat's mushrooms from Ratne and cooking them in a bean casserole for your youngest daughter.

If one believes in the power of right gestures to avert bad luck, what calamity not to have Esta Plat's Old Country mushrooms anymore. Once Esta's shipments stopped arriving, my grandfather's pancreatic cancer bloomed—no more cholent, no more *cronson*, no more Esta. By 1945, my grandfather was dead; a blood tide had washed across the globe; and my mother had run off to Reno to elope with a soldier.

In a 2015 documentary about Chernobyl, *The Babushkas of Chernobyl*, a metal bucket full of freshly gathered forest mushrooms sits on a Ukrainian granny's floor waiting for her to brush the duff and forest debris off the caps. Fist sized, the bolete mushrooms she has picked glow coppery and savory seeming.

Part of a small coterie of women who ignored permanent evacuation orders, the women dubbed Babushkas of Chernobyl, returned to live in the exclusion zone after the Chernobyl nuclear reactor fire and explosion in 1986. Defying the odds of survival in a contaminated atmosphere, one granny explained that she'd always picked these forest mushrooms, always, and she'd continue to pick them, despite their radioactivity far exceeding safety for human consumption. Besides, she needed them for a special dish she served to her other defiant Chernobyl survivor friends on Easter.

Chthonic talismans! Like every mushroom hunter, she knew mushrooms absorb the taste of what lies just below the surface of the soil, the humus dishing up its terrors in a fleshy pileus and stem savory with rain and so much human suffering blended now with burdock, birch, pines, and blackberry canes.

Was this your fate, dear Esta? Gathering radioactive forest mushrooms in Gehenna?

History Lesson

BURIAL PRACTICES

T O COMMEMORATE THE BIRTHS OF SONS LUTZ AND Götz-Hubertus, Josef "Sepp" Dietrich, Hitler's personal chauffeur, asked Heinrich Himmler to be their godfather. According to Jochen Faber in his documentary *The Secret of the Orange Boxes*, after World War II Dietrich spent twelve years of his life sentence in prison, convicted for perpetrating crimes against humanity. His sentence was commuted by a German court in the 1960s, and he lived the remainder of his life in Ludwigsburg, comfortably, on a pension raised for him by former soldiers who took pity on him, because as a war criminal, Dietrich was denied a pension.

In addition to Dietrich's German sentence, he was sentenced to death in absentia by a Russian court for his role in the Donets Campaign, during the Third Battle of Kharkiv (Kharkov), where twenty-three thousand Russian troops lost their lives. In December 1941 to January 1942, Germans in Kharkiv annihilated its Jewish population of fifteen thousand in Drobitsky Yar, a ravine outside Kharkiv. According to Izabella Tabarovsky, German soldiers marched captive Jews from a warehouse where they had been imprisoned, through their former neighborhoods as their Ukrainian neighbors looked on, then shot or shoved Jews alive into the pit in Drobitsky Yar, where they died of exposure if they weren't already dead. A Holocaust memorial was erected at the massacre site in 2002, along with an underground Hall of Memories that records the names of many of the dead. A stone menorah at the site, the Drobitsky Menorah, was shelled on March 26, 2022, by Russian artillery fire, several branches of the stone candelabra obliterated by their ammunition.

At Dietrich's funeral in Ludwigsburg, seven thousand people arrived to mourn their friend, a fallen soldier. When the twenty-five-year lease on his burial plot expired, Dietrich's family declined to renew the lease or claim his headstone. The local stone mason smashed the stone to bits to make the letters illegible, bagged the pieces in several garbage bags, and disposed of the bags at undisclosed locations, so as not to contribute fodder to neo-Nazi relic hunters.

My mother's headstone stood alone at the Rose Hill Cemetery for several years. Though it's common to place small pebbles and stones at the base of headstones to mark a visit to a Jewish loved one's grave, my youngest nephew always leaves pink plastic leis. In summer, my mother's site is often wet from the sprinkler head located nearby. The grass is unusually green around the plot, emerald, like her famous Swedish ivies.

The plot was chosen because of its proximity to Susha's grave. Standing at the foot of my mother's grave and gazing east along the headstone rims, you can almost make out the picture of my grandmother on her stone. Her smile is placid, tight-lipped, her face relaxed, her hair curled neatly around her oval head and parted on the side. She looks so alive in the photo it's disconcerting to catch a glimpse of her.

Dear Susha,

    In my nightmare, the air is thin and hazy. Red sunset. There is smoke somewhere nearby, and fire, but here, there are bees and apple trees. Water fountains. The town square is fifteen times the width of the Street of the Synagogue in Ratno, all the buildings brick. No wood. No smell of mildew. Our home is like Queen Esther's. A string quartet plays music almost every evening. Someone offers me a cookie at my mother's shiva, chocolate, marshmallow center, shortbread base, Head of the Jew.

All Men Are Brothers

RS. K—, THE TURKISH WOMAN WHO LIVED ONE floor above us on Lortzingstraße, favored a Chelsea look: short jacket, mod hat like Yoko Ono wore in the 1960s, boots tucked into her jeans. As she entered the corner liquor store, where I was buying a case of Allgäuer Dunkel beer, she described an attack by a wild swan as she walked on the asphalt pathway along the Neckar River.

"Vicious," she insisted to the clerk, wagging her injured finger, "it pinched me here and wouldn't let go until I kicked it." Her German seemed rushed and confident, asserted with defiance, almost shouted from a mouth full of crooked teeth the color of wet sand. She clenched both fists and twisted them, a gesture I took to mean she wanted to break the swan's neck, and I wondered what it would feel like to punt a hissing swan. I nodded in her direction and looked at the thin blue bruise the swan's beak had made along her pointer, then we three women exchanged a few comments about the sunny but brisk autumn day, the sky already clotted with high clouds that promised rain.

Usually I caught only a glimpse of Mrs. K—'s torso and her arms stretched out above me, or rather a glimpse of her hands clutching her grimy shag carpet as she banged it on the balcony rail above ours, sending the week's detritus from her children's shoes drifting into our living room like the black soot from an incinerator. I also saw her many mornings, from behind, when the weather turned colder, with her white knit muffler wrapped tightly around her neck as she prepared to accompany her youngest son to the Lutheran preschool a few blocks from our apartment, our first of many temporary homes in Ludwigsburg. The boy rode slowly on his bicycle, and she jogged alongside, keeping his speed in check with brusque commands that he pretended not to hear.

Once I glimpsed Mrs. K— in the old, pink stucco center of Ludwigsburg, squabbling at a fruit stall in the farmers market, squeezing tangerines and plucking dates with a tine. She spoke loudly as she punched the air. A few of her countrywomen, in hijab, turned their heads briefly to look at her. She was short and boyish, with a small, sharp-tipped nose, bright brown eyes, brows plucked, penciled, and arched like a skeptic's glare. Her hair was dyed jet black streaked with crimson, and I briefly fantasized that she and I would become friends, practicing our German together as Susha had practiced with her English-speaking daughters around her kitchen table on Newton Street.

Two uncomfortable encounters at the threshold to our apartment squelched this notion, when Mrs. K— held her oldest son, Ahmed, age ten, tightly by the collar, trying to convince us to engage him as our German language tutor. She rubbed her right thumb around the tips of her still injured pointer and middle finger, saying, "*Ein kleines bißchen Geld*" (a little bit of money), offering up a tuition discount for her son's limited language services, complete with that ancient gesture of pawnbrokers, bookies, and beggars, as she rubbed an imaginary coin between her thumb and injured finger.

Ahmed was also the young William Tell who shot rubber-tipped arrows at the apple on his sister's head. They were two-thirds of Mrs. K—'s progeny, the kindergarten boy the third. In the evenings when they were at home, and when Mr. K— was elsewhere, which was often, our ceiling rumbled like a bowling alley, her children's bodies pins awaiting her revolving, heavy, ball: strikes, splits, and spares crashed as Mrs. K—'s hands swept across her daughter's face and body. Curses rose above the melee, the boys curiously silent above our heads, the daughter shrieking, the noise mediated only on the nights when Mr. K— was home, singing softly while he strummed his oud. Each plaintive note was an insufficient salve for his daughter's helplessness and his wife's uncontrollable rage.

Sometimes I'd see Mrs. K— the morning after her daughter's beatings, mod hat cocked at a jaunty angle, and she would smile and wave, greeting her neighbors with frisky, overly earnest gestures. I'd also see the daughter with her older brother as they began their walk to school, when I was returning from the neighborhood bakery with pumpkin seed rolls or a sweet cheese tart covered with cherries and streusel. I never learned the girl's name, but during that winter's one meager snowstorm the little girl spent the afternoon with her brothers wielding soupspoons to gather up all the snow in our courtyard. They built a snowman with a carrot nose and buttons down his portly chest that the girl had ripped off her mother's blouse left hanging on the clothesline in the storm.

As a child, I loved the heavy snows of Denver winters. My mother slogged through backyard drifts to form the grid for our fox and chickens game, she the fox, prowling at the edge of one of the pie-shaped wedges she had circumscribed inside the circle, me in the center, shivering on a tiny patch of tamped down snow with my younger sister, trapped as the fox licked its bloody muzzle, waiting for its prey to fumble. My mother tired easily of this game, the cold, the silly repetitions of grabbing the backs of our coats and shaking us until we screamed, and so would often leave us stranded in the circle, one foot in front of the next stepping in her larger prints, listening to the muffled echo of the back door slamming, dreading her bark to come inside. When the yard stilled to the dampened hush of falling snow, the momentary quiet mocked the aftermath of our mother's barked goodbye. We held out our tongues to snowflakes, gazing up at the thick sky and falling shapes, the infinity of unique and perfect crystals melting on our coats, our lashes, our mittens.

In her youth, my mother was taller than Mrs. K— and strong as an ox. She had many bowling trophies, which I dusted. Blond, blue-eyed, "a bombshell," my father once observed. Marlene Dietrich was my mother's idol, Dietrich's sultry pouts my mother's practiced ones, her chilly gaze, her perfect statue's hips and breasts. It didn't take a malicious theft of my mother's buttons for a snowman's coat to feel her slaps or the sting of her tongue. It didn't take any provocation whatsoever, and so my younger sister and I learned to shield our heads from her wooden paddle's blows. Crouched in front of her, if our crossed wrists protecting our heads had shattered instead of bruised, who would have thought such a siren, such an agile, perfect beauty, such a bright angel capable of harm? Even when her paddle splintered the locked door my sister and I had placed between her and us, bruised our shoulders and our arms, our father, Susha, and our teachers all pretended not to notice. Parental rage was nothing new in those days. It flowed logically from war.

Like Mrs. K—, who loved pistachio-filled *lokum*, Turkish gelatin candy, my mother had a sweet tooth, so those who didn't know her thought it transferred to her disposition. To those who thought they knew her well, she was her mother's daughter. At Frost Bakery, she laughed and chatted with the clerks, who plied her with extra in her baker's dozen bag: bagels for my father's Sunday brunch, *eier kichlach* for Susha's coffee klatch with her daughters and daughter-in-law on Saturday afternoons, apple strudel doled out to us in little slices if we were silent and invisible and never, ever asked about the Old Country or Esta Plat.

A month before Christmas, the central square of Ludwigsburg is transformed into a launching pad whose destination is the kingdom of heaven. Cranes hoist twenty-foot-high gilded angels, their forms elongated nudes with wings, and cables anchor them to the light posts in Market Plaza. Praising "Hallelujah!" their arms are raised high above their heads, their bodies poised to surge into the stratosphere.

With the angels comes the *Weihnachtsmarkt*, with its booths and goods, and vendors, and a few weeks before Christmas, a handful of beggars.

Sitting cross-legged on a towel, one frail man positioned himself at the southeast corner of the Lutheran church, his small, wooden alms bowl placed at a forty-five-degree angle from his bent left knee. His eyes were close-set, with thick brows and lashes, his head a narrow oval, buzz-cut hair, pointed chin. His brow and jaw seemed disproportionate on his long neck, skeletal arms and legs. He resembled a village man I'd seen in a televised report from the BBC late that autumn, the man beating the ground with a broom made of sticks then wadding up the placket of his jacket in despair while a hazmat team, hooded and dressed all in white, rushed through his flock of chickens and turkeys. The men gathered the fowls for destruction, to prevent the spread of what was then thought to become a pandemic avian flu. The footage followed the condemned livestock to the truck that carted them away, feathers floating through the air, then a camera pan of the man's packed-mud yard, now empty except for his concrete hut, his twig and twine fences destroyed in the melee. The man's body seemed to wither as the camera continued to roll, just as the beard and hair of the frail, begging man turned from deep black to a dull, steel gray as he sat in front of the Ludwigsburg church on successively colder days.

Twice a week my husband and I passed the seated, begging man, as we wound through the temporary maze of Christmas booths on our way to evening German language classes. The man stared like an eroded statue, around him the aroma of grilling meat, the lavender and myrrh of the Christmas season, the riot of whirligigs and jingling earrings waiting to be purchased at many booths. Once I saw the begging man smile as he watched children squeal aboard the miniature Ferris wheel at the east end of the Christmas market. As the days grew colder and the humidity rose, he became abject, kneeling on a small, thin cushion, arms stretched out in front of him, forehead touching the ground. Only then, when his body was almost prone on the cold ground and our gaze hungered for divinity fudge, did his wooden alms bowl hold a few coins.

Our *Volkshochschule*, German-language night-school class was full of former enemies—a Frenchman and an Algerian, a Senegalese woman about to marry a German; a Pole, two Russians, an Albanian and a Christian Kosovar, Turks and Kurds, religious and secular. One Thai woman abandoned in Germany by her German boyfriend had been disfigured when he threw acid on her face, and mostly during class she sat silent, confused, staring at her hands, picking at her cuticles. My husband and I, not refugees in our generation, sat across the room from a Vietnamese welder and his wife, ages fifty-two and forty-nine, respectively, starting their lives again in the state of Baden-Württemberg along with their four children.

Once we'd startled a night-school classmate who worked as a janitor at the university where we taught by day. We discovered her pushing her housekeeping cart toward the women's restroom near the library, and she stopped, confused by our presence out of context. "Vanapei," I said, shifting the strap of my black briefcase so that I could extend my hand to shake hers. She noted our heavy, cashmere coats, our polished shoes, our leather gloves. The colleague we'd been chatting with looked from her to us, surprised. In general, professors spoke to one another, and to students during class or office conferences. With office staff, it seemed, exchanges were more stratified, and with staff like janitors and groundskeepers, cashiers in the lunchroom, only polite hellos. The ambience before the holidays relaxed when bags of chocolates passed from hand to hand, cookies doled, glühwein poured during after-hours parties, and yet the old class barriers remained in place. We were reminded once or twice that language acquisition was handled at the university in accelerated classrooms meant for students, or with private tutors. Had we tried the Goethe Institute, one colleague asked. We had. Night-school classes were geared for immigrating laborers and asylum seekers and the language set they'd need. At that time, the state placed no restrictions on who could attend, though now those rules have changed. Allowances were made for our naivete, but we offered no apologies.

As we walked across Ludwigsburg in the evening to attend this class, down Schorndorfer Straße and through the heart of Ludwigsburg's central plaza, I imagined Susha riding the streetcar down West Colfax Avenue to attend English classes at the Emily Griffith Night School when she was little more than a frightened teenaged girl. Though I could see a body moving in an overcoat and climbing aboard the streetcar, I could barely access Susha's mind. She spoke Yiddish at home, and while in Ratne Russian and Ukrainian flecked with Polish, though she didn't read Cyrillic. She read Hebrew and Esta's letters. She never mastered English fluency, and her daughters made fun of her pronunciation behind her back. I remember the embarrassment and shame I felt when I discovered that Susha couldn't help me spell "Thousand Island dressing" for a class assignment or "Sophie," her English name, without a coach looking over her shoulder and voicing every letter in her good right ear. And Esta Plat? Dear Esta, the spelling of your name is a transliteration from words that brought my mother only heartache after Susha's avalanche of grief.

There was urgency and fatigue among our *Volkshochschule* colleagues. For them, learning another language wasn't fun. For them, learning another language wasn't even like drinking a green smoothie with arugula or seeking out other nasty-tasting foods to keep their faces supple. For them, attendance was required along the asylum path they were pursuing. For us, the class was a reminder of the barely scalable language wall blocking access to a better life in Baden-Württemberg. Everyone in the room would gladly have traded places with us, though they all knew America's open door has long been mostly closed to laborers like them.

We didn't introduce Vanapei to our university colleague or press her with our greeting. She removed one blue rubber glove to tuck a loose strand of hair behind her ear, shook our hands tepidly, then pushed off with her cart to clean another restroom. Our colleague later said he recognized her; she cleaned his office, though they never spoke. One evening in class I'd spoken in Chinese with her, because she told us classmates that she'd owned a restaurant in Taipei with her former husband. I had taught English in Taichung City, I said. Those Chinese words confused and flustered her, so I switched back to German. She never really spoke to me again. Why she was in Germany, we never learned, and the one time my husband and I had turns in class to explain to everyone what we do for a living, we simply said we teach. No, we said, we weren't asylum seekers.

Frau Claudia, our caustic, skinny German teacher, was in an uncharacteristically good mood as she greeted us on the last night of class before the Christmas holiday. Usually chain-smoking outside in the cement courtyard before class, she busied herself this night with her student teacher, Petra, the two of them ferrying bags of groceries for our party, her folder stuffed with cut-out images of beer and scotch bottles, her favorite brand of *Sekt*, gin, and chardonnay, also vodka, ouzo, and anisette, all props for the dialogue exercise we were going to practice to boost our vocabulary, our sociability, our general conviviality, asking questions of our Muslim classmates, designated for the classroom skit as grocery clerks, as we filled our imaginary shopping carts full of discounted liquor for the holidays.

"Is it cheap, with a discount, or is it still expensive?" I smiled at Serpil and waited for her answer while she adjusted her turquoise-blue chador.

"Yes, we have no discount on that brandy," Ahmed answered in her stead, "would you like to see another kind?"

Secular Ida, from Istanbul, continued. "Do you prefer hefeweizen or Chablis?"

Lumya, an Albanian with private allegiances and a language sense all her own, replied, "No, thank you, corkscrew pretty, dozen have already my."

"Vodka, vodka!" our classmate Ossip said again, tapping his forehead with rough stonemason's fingers as he waited for Oleg, the Russian carpenter, to respond.

Ossip preferred schnapps flavored with Black Forest cherries, and he drank it from a silver flask while sitting in his red Mazda during breaks. In class, he sat between me and Serpil, on his left. His gray hair was always neatly parted, glasses shiny and pressed back on his nose, his leathery cheeks freshly shaven, a gold crucifix necklace prominently displayed on top of his maroon sweater vest. His black slacks had a military crease, black shoes buffed lustrous, and a black notebook held his writing paper, which he seldom used. The only sign of day labor was his scabbed and swollen knuckles, bruised fingers, tips stained, cracked, but never dirty.

While we usually practiced the mundane skills of filling out job applications, giving the addresses to our dismal concrete apartment blocks or asking for city maps at tourist bureaus, where it was imagined in our textbooks we ventured on the weekends, this night before Christmas the simple past tense appeared in a long, declined column on the chalkboard. Suddenly, with a vehicle to voice our active past, chalk was handed around, our little sticks of TNT. We doodled superimposed political maps over the map of a united Germany, Kwan his Vietnam and Oleg his former home in Georgia, Ida her Turkey and Marguerite her Senegal, but what could any of us say to one another about the actions of our governments in our behalf? Frau Claudia watched us for a moment then clapped her hands as though we were a kennel of rabid dogs. We looked up, salivated. She wrote the date, 15 *Dezember*, and we copied in our notebooks. She drew a cruciform on the blackboard and I thought we were going to hear an explanation of the birth of Christ to bolster our vocabulary, but she had drawn the cruciform to construct a chart on which to list categories of fruit and nuts, the ingredients of our Christmas feast.

On we marched, to slice a basket full of real fruit. Petra placed a cloth shopping bag on the table, displayed an array of Wüsthof knives, four 3½-inch paring blades and one imposing chef's knife with its tang of gleaming steel. There was a scuffle as the men grabbed for the knives, shouts in Turkish between Kemal and Ahmed, as Ossip's large and muscled hand quickly closed around the handle of the longest blade. He swished it through the air with a commanding snap of his wrist, holding the knife point perpendicular to his body, daring all challengers.

Our other Russian classmate, Nicoli, arrived in the doorway just as the swordsmen armed, the overhead fluorescent lights glinting off the white frosting of his wife's five-layer, raspberry-filled yellow cake. The layers had shifted en route to the party, the frosting cracked. He stopped in the doorway and discreetly pushed the top layer of his listing tower back toward the center of the plate while eyes focused on the men holding knives.

Kemal and Ahmed each grabbed a paring knife and one each went to my husband and Kwan. Ossip stepped sideways, his back to the wall, head half-turned, watching Kemal's and Ahmed's hands.

With three large strides, Ossip was at the small utility sink in the corner of the room, where Frau Claudia sometimes rinsed the dirty sponge she used to clean the chalkboards.

The rest of us pretended to be busy, pushing our long desks together into one huge rectangle, the classroom reconfigured for us newly christened knights. Steel clanged in short, zealous intervals, as Ossip worked the knife blade against a honing steel, the room silent except for the sickening sound of steel meeting steel. His lips were tight as he plucked a gray hair and sliced it with the blade. Dissatisfied, he stropped again, then plucked another hair, a slash, a test, until the knife split a hair evenly down the sloughed cells of its shaft. Petra looked at Frau Claudia. Frau Claudia looked at my husband, tallest in the room, but he was holding a puny paring knife. She looked at Kwan, who was watching Ossip's scabby knuckles. Kemal and Ahmed lowered their eyes and smiled at one another, but what did their smile mean?

No fruit in sight, Kemal picked up the knife by its handle and flung it, with a powerful flip of his wrist, into the wooden cutting board on the table in front of him, timing his throw with the clash of Ossip's knife against the honing steel. The blade penetrated the wood with a *thwuck*, like the sound of a raw chicken breast separating from the bone. Ossip watched Kemal's hands. Kemal, holding tightly to the knife handle, removed it from the cutting board. Ahmed flicked his knife. It struck the board but fell away.

Ossip sped the tempo of his stropping. Ahmed tossed his knife again, so hard the blade tip disappeared into the cutting board. For a third time, Frau Claudia called the kings, "Ossip, Kemal, Ahmed!" trying to raise her raspy voice above the song of knives.

Ossip balanced the knife between the hot and cold faucet handles on the sink. He lined the honing steel along the edge of the metal sink and took a handkerchief from his pocket, which he used to slowly wipe the sweat from his brow and cheeks. My husband

stepped to the sink, and Ossip picked up the handle and caressed
the blade edge with his thumb. He hesitated, this man with whom
we could barely converse or give directions as he offered one rainy
night to drive us home through the dark back streets of Ludwigsburg; this man who would come to rely on the charity of his oldest
daughter one month after this party, when he fell off a scaffolding
at work and broke his back.

Ossip offered up the knife, handle pointing out. Ahmed and Kemal stopped playing their knife-tossing game. Serpil, her voice ring-
ing with false cheer, told the class her father was a diplomat in Paris.
Marcello, from Portugal, a mechanic at the Daimler plant near
Stuttgart, walked around our desks, awarding all of us with small
red felt stars Frau Claudia had cut out for our party. Lumia lit the
votive candles in the center of the table, but the still-lit match she
tossed into the utility sink missed its mark and set a wastebasket full
of our botched holiday greeting cards on fire. The men all rushed to
put the fire out before the smoke alarm went off, and then the class
was over.

After many mugs of glühwein at the Christmas fair, we arrived in
our dimly lit courtyard on Lortzingstraße after class. Mrs. K— was
smoking on the apartment stoop, and the ember from her cigarette
tip moved up and down in a jittery line, from her lips down to her
knees. When she smoked, she often liked to pace on the sidewalk beyond the front door stoop and sometimes stripped the leaves from
the privet hedge that lined the courtyard. The top layer of the hedge
across from the stoop was bare, and this night she held her cigarette
slack, dangling her arm along her side. She wasn't wearing her mod
hat, and her coat was unzipped, though it was cold outside. Her
white turtleneck sweater was pulled up to the middle of her chin.
Upstairs, her little girl was yelling at her brothers. Mrs. K— blew a
smoke ring and watched as the tight ring dissipated into the night
sky. When she flicked her ashes, they fell onto the stoop, and she
smudged them with her toe. The dead grosbeak we'd seen in the dirt

underneath the hydrangeas in the courtyard was still there, where I'd seen it earlier, a victim of age, weather, bird flu, or perhaps the arrow tip of William Tell. In life, it had been so fat it seemed about to burst as it flitted from feeder to feeder on the balconies above the courtyard, recipient of so much tenderness and care.

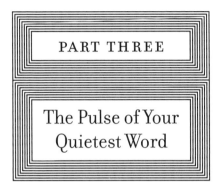

PART THREE

The Pulse of Your
Quietest Word

My Aleph

FTER A YEAR'S WAIT, I RECEIVED A RESPONSE FROM
the Arolsen Archives in Bad Arolsen, Germany, "To our
regret, our search has failed to yield . . ." Among the mention of cottage industries developed in post–World War I Ratne is
one for forest mushrooms, no mention of Esta Plat, and the longest
list of entrepreneurial women in the Ratne Yizkor book, names recited from memory by a Ratne survivor in Tel Aviv who may have
emigrated many years before World War II, is associated with
women selling eggs, challah, and bottled seltzer water.

In the Buenos Aires phonebook, there are several Ratners listed,
several Plats. Before I left for Israel, my son and my son-in-law
called many, to see if they had relatives who had lived in Ratne. The
last was Salomon Plat, a Holocaust survivor from Łódź. He didn't
know other people from the Jewish community in Buenos Aires,
he said, though they lived all around him, one family on his block.
My son-in-law, a native Spanish speaker, said Salomon was reticent to speak, depressed, that after the war he'd moved from country to country without rooting anywhere. The Łódź ghetto was liq-
uidated in 1944, but in 1942, some Jews were removed and sent

to Auschwitz and Chełmno to die. Before the 1939 invasion, thousands of Jews fled Łódź and so perhaps Salomon Plat was among those. He would have been a child of eleven in 1939.

Before the questions ended, Salomon Plat muffled his sobs, and my son-in-law felt cruel descending unannounced into the consciousness of Salomon Plat in order to make him remember what he had spent a lifetime trying to forget.

The results were always similar: no comment, no memory, *I closed and locked that door*. One woman, no relation, said she was a very little girl when she left Ratne and she remembered it as a beautiful, delightful village.

In Israel, in addition to boiled eggs, almost every part of the chicken is served in grilled dishes, including heart at nonkosher restaurants. I learned this at the one restaurant open on Friday evening near our hotel on King George Street, where David and I dined after a shuttle ride from Ben Gurion Airport, ushered into the city graced by rain, complete with thunder and lightning bolts that lit the sky all the way from Tel Aviv to Jerusalem. I thought it was an omen, mostly good. The woman sitting next to me wept during the crowded shuttle ride, overjoyed, I thought, to be in Israel, though it turned out her husband was stepping on her swollen foot.

The next morning, we walked underneath electrical wires crisscrossing the narrow lanes in Jerusalem's Old City, laundry lines strung below them. At the Jaffa Gate, plainclothes policemen loitered, attempting nonchalance, pretending interest in storefronts displaying wares they saw every day—brass pots and Moroccan leather goods, censers, Armenian ceramics glazed in vivid blues. At the crossroad near the Western Wall, the Kotel, a guide with a Brookline accent, "giddy with happiness," she said, turned to her charges, our cue to avoid the jam of tourists and duck down a blind alley at the entrance to a former abbey now called King David's Tomb.

Past the maze of anterooms, many of them walled off, the cenotaph represents the site ascribed during the Middle Ages as King David's burial site. An elevated wooden coffin draped in blue velvet sets the mood, covered with a sheet of plastic like the plastic covering the good couches in the living rooms of bubbies' houses across the world. A young woman, small prayer book nestled in her hands, glared as my husband and I whispered jokes about the plastic cover, but she misunderstood our irreverent mirth. We were channeling bubbies' approval of a plastic sheet draped over the coffin cover to protect the velvet from all that desert dust and grit.

The low ceilings softened the movement of people throughout the tomb. In an instant, a small adjoining courtyard filled with Israeli army recruits, mostly men, two in the light olive-green uniforms of soldiers, the rest in jeans and T-shirts. The sudden clatter of semiautomatic rifles slung casually like toy guns over their shoulders sounded like metal dominoes as the new recruits packed into the courtyard during their requisite tour of Jerusalem's Old City.

The potential of rapid-fire weapons in so small a space tasted like regurgitated gall. Suddenly, there was no air to breathe; suddenly, the only smell imagined smoke, the only sound ricocheting bullets. The recruits ignored us, but we could not ignore them, their guns, their ammunition clips. The instantaneous surround of soldiers sobered and sickened. Faith, spectacle, and the show of force made the tomb seem even more ludicrous. We hesitated a few minutes after the recruits departed, blocked from exiting the tomb by the bearded, stooped, and pale caretaker who stood in inside the doorway, shaking the charity box. We tossed in a few shekels and fled.

The Central Archives for the History of the Jewish People promised on its 2014 website to be an archive of important materials for eastern European ancestry research not catalogued at the YIVO Institute in New York City, accessible only live then, no online rec-

ords, no appointments necessary. English speakers welcome, which
I had understood to mean I didn't need to hire a translator to accompany me.

Situated on the edge of a ravine at the periphery of Hebrew University, in a mobile unit in "High Tech Village," the location of the
archives was unknown to the reference librarians in the main campus library. They hadn't heard of High Tech Village, either, nor was
High Tech Village on the main campus map. After several phone
calls and two bum steers, David and I found the anchored trailer we
were looking for in a regimented row of trailers once used as wom-
en's dorms.

Before I began my search, the center's director cautioned that
because Esta Plat was "not important," like a mayor or a rabbi, a philanthropist, a union organizer, or "successful," he said, like a busi-
nesswoman, but rather "just a housewife," my search would likely
be futile.

"But," he added, smiling as he leaned back in his chair. He tilted
forward and his chair legs banged against the floor as he wiped the
lenses of his filmy glasses. "Here you are in Eretz Yisrael! What
could be better than that?" He held up four fingers. "You have
your own memory of Esta's letters; you said you held them in your
hands."

In my hands. Yes, I held them.

*I have my mother's words, Esta's name spoken more than once, Esta
Plat.*

*I have pages of testimony from Yad Vashem memorializing the
deaths of Plats and Plots, a few of those from Ratno, one testimony
from a Plat survivor near Tel Aviv. I should be satisfied there are Plats
among the living, but I have have not found what I am looking for,
dear Esta.*

"How much do you want! A report card? A diploma? Was your
Esta noted for her scholarship? Do you think you're going to find

a stack of scrapbooks from a treasure chest in Ratne? After Hitler? After Stalin?"

I want a birth certificate signed by God.

He shook his head. "Someone will come forward with more documents from shtetlach when they think the time is right. It's impossible to know what people stole. People steal! They steal! That's all. For now, four sources. It's an important number. Be happy. Your Esta wasn't one of the four Matriarchs, after all."

I thought about an artifact I'd seen in the Israel Museum, Pontius Pilate's name carved on a block of stone repurposed as a lintel in a Roman theater, the only extant physical archeological record of Pontius Pilate's name carved on a piece of stone. The stone was on exhibit along with troves of physical evidence from Herod I's rule, glazed blue tiles from Herod's baths and preserved remnants of Herod's favorite foods, jars of preserved anchovies, figs, olive oil, and wine, imported for him from Spain and stored in the Herodium, nautical knots from the port at Caesarea Maritima, a rusting anchor.

Relics are the provenance of kings, if they escape wholesale pillaging and liquidation. They exist because they were buried or hidden from sight or some group deemed them valuable. What better place is there in Judeo-Christian culture than Jerusalem to encounter what has been preserved for public discourse and what destroyed, to witness how the past is ignored, revered, revised, revisited, reclaimed, removed. Where you, dear Esta, remain invisible.

The director was pleasant and earnest, his white-and-blue crocheted yarmulke clipped at an angle to his dark, curly hair. His desk job had thickened his middle, his gait measured as he walked me down the hallway past offices crammed floor to ceiling with dusty books stuffed with loose papers and photographs, desks piled high with newspapers and magazines, coffee mugs with brown stain rings, more dust, yellow flakes of dried binder's glue, encyclopedias, volumes whose cracked spines and embossed letters were too faded or worn to read. My eyes locked on a knee-high pile of newspapers from a town wiped off the map, papers still waiting to be perused that might, for someone, reveal the mundane path of many common lives made irrelevant by their unrecorded deeds.

The director handed me off to a man hunkered over a desk far too small for him, behind him a wooden card catalog, also miniature, with drawers whose faded yellow index cards referenced the books, ephemera, journals, and newspapers in the archive that had actually been filed away. When I saw the small size of the catalog and the offices in disarray, my heart sank.

The archivist pressed his hands to his forehead to avert his next headache, me. He didn't look up from his desk as the director introduced me. He didn't offer his hand to shake, nor did I offer mine.

"You won't find anything there," he said, pointing to the card catalog. "Nothing's in English." He scooted his chair back and placed both palms on the edge of his desk to lift himself up. "Can you read Russian? Polish? Hebrew? Yiddish?" He pursed his lips as though someone had slipped a few sour deer turds into the bowl of chocolate-covered raisins he nibbled at his desk.

"What kind of name is Plat? Platt? Plätt? Plot. It's a stupid name. A non-name. A nothing name, like all the other nothing names uneducated Jews gave themselves. Flower. Almond. Onion. Stone." He waved one big hand above his disheveled gray hair, his wedding ring strangling his swollen finger.

"And what did she do, this Esta Plat of yours? Was she a teacher? A communist? A labor organizer? Did she run a reeducation camp for young women about to make aliyah to the Holy Land? Did she teach the ladies of Ratne how to drive a tractor?"

He fished a piece of trash from his basket and wrote the Hebrew letters *peh* and *bet* on the back of a wrinkled sheet of paper in the fast running style of a Hebrew native speaker. "See," he said, punching at the paper.

To the ear, *peh* and *bet* sound almost interchangeable, like *P* and *B* in English. He poked at the letters with his forefinger. "Have you seen *Plat* written? Plat is nothing. Plat? A place, a person who lives in a place. Esta Person-Who-Lives-in-a-Place. So, what else is new?" He sighed, throttle wide, letting his engine build up steam.

"Blatt, we know from German," he said. "Blatt is sheet, like a sheet of paper, or leaf. Paper makes sense. Plat is nothing. Place. Place dweller. Who takes a name like that?"

The archivist took out a roll of microfilm and threaded it through an ancient reader the size of a VW bug. "You might find something in a *Pinkas* book, who knows? We photographed some pages from Ratne. Plat, Blatt," he said as he spun the film rapidly through the viewer. "Maybe there's a bill of sale in Kovel' or Lutsk, maybe a court record for a dispute of some kind. Maybe her man sold a goat, or someone stole her chickens, and the town historian made a record." He shook his head and twisted his watch around his wrist before he checked the time. "Jews were Jews. They lived here and there. Their lives lasted from sunup until sundown, and that was all. Nothing remarkable, no *Mashiach* (Messiah) rescued them."

He pointed to imaginary spots on an imaginary map. "Not every little town kept exacting records. The farther from a big town, the less there is. Do you want to look?"

Of course, I wanted to look, but after his preamble, what was I looking for, exactly? I scanned inches and inches of the film that supposedly contained ephemera from the entire province of Volyn, more than five centuries of ephemera, on it blurred letters photographed quickly with a poor camera, small scraps of paper torn, decomposing, or burned, with faded names and notations in Hebrew and Yiddish, numerals for quantities of zlotys or rubles, long columns with names or phrases written haphazardly in all directions on the page. If there were a mention or a record of a Plat or a Blatt, I'd gloss right over it.

"Could you look," I said, bracing for another rant.

"Could I look?" The archivist looked up at the ceiling and rolled his eyes. "Could I look?" he asked the throng of invisible researchers. "How about him," the archivist said, pointing to David sitting at a long table by the window, writing in a small pocket notebook he carried in the breast pocket of his shirt, his personal, portable *Pinkas* book.

"He doesn't read Hebrew," I said.

The archivist shook his head and drummed on the side of the microfilm reader. "Or Russian. Or Polish." My husband didn't look up from his notebook. "Why haven't you been here before now," he asked. "What kind of Jews are you?"

The woman who had helped to found the center over fifty years ago had joined the search and offered a few kind observations to mitigate the archivist's nasty ones. The search for families with origins in eastern Europe has evolved since the dissolution of the Soviet Union and the extension of EU membership to countries in the former Soviet Bloc. I didn't discuss the politics of archives or what wealthy donors and governments can accomplish, free-market translator entrepreneurs. I didn't share gushing anecdotes about the archives we'd found with information about my husband's family in Vilnius. The state of things was clear enough standing in the trailer gazing at a card catalog smaller than the branch library card catalog I perused as a girl at the Cherry Creek branch library in Denver.

The center's founder was familiar with the organization of Ratners who emigrated to Israel in the 1930s, but the organization has since disbanded. She cuffed her colleague on his beefy shoulder, I assumed to remind him that not everyone would appreciate his prickles.

He waved her hand away. "Never mind, let's take a look," he said. He placed his hand on the film crank and spun it like a roulette wheel. Lists, files, receipts, bits of paper categorized, some not, test papers, crude maps, rosters from conscription, tax records, Hebrew school attendees, synagogue members, records of legal proceedings, years, phrases, and names whizzed by in an almost straight black line.

Two young Haredi men reading old newspaper clippings and an American expatriot in dark purple sweat clothes researching a massacre in Lithuania came to stand behind us, momentarily curious. "There," he said, pointing as the reel slowed to a stop, "and there. In scraps from Ratne. A Blatt and a Blatt. Philanthropic contributions to the Yeshiva in Vilnius. Your Blatt was generous. Congratulations. I'll make you pictures to take home. We close in twenty minutes."

My cheeks burned; the base of my skull pounded. The American woman in purple put her hand on my arm while the archivist attended to the copies in another room and wrote the invoice for me to pay a few shekels for them. "It's not so hard to teach yourself to read Polish," she said. "I did it in just under six months so that I could search these archives myself."

"Did you find what you were looking for," I asked.

"Everyone finds something," she said.

Photocopied images of two partial slips of paper from 1934 with Mendel Blat's name on them in Yiddish weighed heavy in my briefcase. The first night of Hanukkah was about to begin, and when we returned to the hotel, the desk clerk recited a version of the holiday for neophytes and after invited us to the candle-lighting ceremony of the "nine-branched candelabra called a *hanukkiah*," he said, chased by *sufganiyot*, jam-filled jelly doughnuts like the bismarks Susha bought from Mildred's Kosher Grocery. We thanked him for the holiday overview and the invitation and left the cramped lobby, spent the dusk and early dark peering into restaurants near Zion Square, where large families had gathered to celebrate the holiday together. A young huckster corralled us into his small subterranean café, boasting that he served the best falafel in Jerusalem. Once we were served, his only customers, two of his friends peered inside the door and summoned him to the square outside to light his *hanuk-kiah*. "Excuse me," he said, beginning the requisite recitation about the festival of Hanukkah for his supposed gentile guests.

"No need to explain," David said, "we know." Having pushed the best falafel in Jerusalem to the far side of his plate, he turned to the greasy french fries and doused them with ketchup. He stared over-long at the goopy red. "Couldn't you let yourself believe you have enough? Mendel Blat was Esta's husband? Or brother? Or someone close?"

The Ester Liba Plat on two pages of testimony from Yad Vashem was a murdered child from a village not far from Warsaw, daughter of murdered Lea Futerman Plat born in 1911, several years after Susha and her family emigrated. I've seen Mendel Blat's name throughout the Ratne Yizkor book and on the necrology list at Yad Vashem. He was born a few years after my grandmother, and maybe when he was a boy he threw dirt clods at Susha and Esta from the corner of his block. Mendel Blat hat maker, artisan, respected citizen of Ratne. He embraced the changes brought by the twentieth century and applied them to his village. He was a philanthropist, and like Esta, he likely stood along Market Street in Ratne waving a Polish flag when Poland took over the administration of Ratne in 1920. Maybe he was Ratne's brand of optimistic stoic, thinking pogroms might end. Maybe he thought the pogrom the town had just endured, or the next, or the next, would be the last. Ratne's kosher butcher, Rebe Abba Plot, lost his fingers then his life in the pogrom of 1920. The massacred in 1942 included Yitzchak Plot, his wife Reitza, daughter Bracha Plot/ Plat and her unnamed children. Is Reitza you, dear Esta, hiding in the cherished name my grandmother called you by?

Poles stabilized the muddy roads leading into and out of Ratne, cobbled some. Narrow plank footbridges remained throughout the bog, and in winter, when the mud froze over, hearty Ratne youth like Mendel Blat smiled at the cameraman recording the town's modern sense of self, its citizens with mostly clean, dry feet, the women in cotton stockings they wished were silk, the men in tailored pants, no scolding rebbes with side curls and patriarchal beards calling out the sinful, modern ways of the town's remaining youthful population.

Ratne was on the rape-and-pillage highway throughout medieval and early modern history. Twentieth-century Ratne had a more secular Tarbut school, which taught among its subjects Russian, Polish, Yiddish, Hebrew, and natural science. In addition to the institutions Mendel Blat administered, three or four Zionist and Zionist-youth organizations formed cohorts and political parties, while the local communist party cell met in an undisclosed basement in the village.

Handsome Mendel Blat, high forehead, thick, wavy hair, always captured on film with the same shocked look, eyes wide, mouth ajar as though he'd seen Hashem. In one photograph, his winter coat is tailored, wool, under it a suit of stylish cut. Mendel Blat of charitable giving, a modern, progressive man. Some might have called him a mensch.

Mendel Blat helped found Ratne's first Jewish administered bank, the Popular Jewish Bank, opened in 1923 and closed in 1939. The route away from Ratne was via Kamin'-Kashyrs'kyi, to the forest, and on toward Sarny and Kyiv. Avraham Barg, a Ratne survivor, said no one thought to flee in 1939, because the Jews of Ratne reasoned, who would bother to kill the Jews?

Two photocopied sheets from the Central Archives for the History of the Jewish People, file number HM3/291.4, could they be my aleph? My aleph! Paid for with eleven shekels, sitting on my bookshelf in a plastic sleeve! Proof of something! But what?

Not Jorge Luis Borges's Aleph, a fictive magic orb that held the essence of all life and death and mystery, or even an infinite corri-

dor of mirrors reflecting aleph, the first letter in the Hebrew alphabet, the first letter in one of the names of God, a letter that has no
sound and yet all sounds. Instead, I held two photocopied sheets
with thirty-three entries on one sheet, twenty-eight on the next,
script nearly illegible, their words chanting generosity, spirit, faith,
a vast network of Jewish life far outstripping Ratne, if only I could
let myself believe!

When I listen closely to the photocopied sheets whispering in
my study, they say, *Vilnius, Vilnius!* and when I hold them in both
fists, it isn't an image of the unknowable you that I see, dear Esta, or
handsome Mendel Blat, or all the dead of Ratne, but rather, urbane
Vilnius on three snowy February nights where my husband and I
held each other close like the young lovers we once were! The seat
of Jewish learning, a Sanhedrin in the Baltics, the Jerusalem of the
North! O! The once Great Synagogue that nurtured the legendary
Vilna Gaon! That Vilnius! The Vilnius that fed my husband and
me strawberry blintzes in an Italian Renaissance–style grotto and
cream of forest mushroom soup and goulash with too much pepper, the Vilnius that warmed our hands at the imagined druidic fire
ring in the forest above Gediminas's fortress walls. The Vilnius that
on another seemingly beautiful summer day in 1940 sheltered No-
bel laureate Czesław Miłosz in cafe Literatų Svetainė on Gediminas
Avenue while "dusty" Soviet tanks "with their little turrets," as Mi-
losz recollects in his autobiography *Native Realm*, entered town to
begin their occupation of Lithuania.

A bronze bust of the Gaon, the revered rabbi of Vilnius (1720–
1797), stood on a pedestal on a narrow path near the site of the
Great Synagogue, now an empty lot with an info-stele covered in
graffiti, where nearby a group of friends smoked tobacco from a
hookah. When linguist Chatzkel Lemchen and the few other Jews
who survived the liquidation of the Vilnius ghetto came back to
resettle in Vilnius after World War II, they were grudgingly given
a bust of the Gaon to commemorate the survival of their culture.

Folklore claimed the bust was really a flawed cast of Stalin's head someone foisted off onto Vilnius's Jewish survivors. My husband remembers this tale as a bust of Lenin, but really the bust looked more like Marx to me.

Even though community members knew the bust was a piece of metal dusted off from the basement of a storeroom in the Kremlin, they accepted the gift, so called. That is the nature of belief. Borges never says at the conclusion of "The Aleph" if he actually saw the Aleph or only dreamed it or kept the vision of the sacred orb a secret to spite a rival.

History Lesson

RESISTANCE AND CULTURE

K AREL BERKHOFF LISTED TOWNS NEAR RATNE THAT planned armed resistance once the Reichkommissariat established their administrations: Dubrovytsia, Sarny, Sosnove, Volodymyrets, Kovel', district seat for Ratne, and Dubno. Jewish councils called the Order Service forced the younger men to stop "that kind of planning," urged appeasement at all costs, reasoning that resistance was futile anyway, and cooperation might save some lives. Members of the council extorted food from village families for Nazi quotas of wheat, beat people and kidnapped women and children to meet the labor quotas the Nazis had imposed on villages in the area.

In the summer of 1942, after the massacre in Ratne, there was an uprising in nearby Kremenets' in August, Tuchyn in September, and Mizoch in October, and though two thousand Jews escaped from Tuchyn before its liquidation, most of those who fled to the woods didn't survive; they were pursued and shot.

According to oral history, Mendel Plotzker, my kinsman, no wife named, practiced glazing as his trade. The oldest of his three sons, Simcha, translation *happy*, had served in the Polish-Soviet

War. Simcha knew how to fight and shoot a gun. He proposed to
resist the slavish labor that he, his father, and three brothers were
subject to in nearby Zabolottya, labor forced on all the artisans of
Ratne whose skills were useful somehow to the Nazis' administration, though no one was replacing windows just then. Simcha reasoned that even though it was foolhardy to resist a well-organized
army, it was better to resist than surrender.

This was 1941, and the massacre outside of Kyiv in the ravine
called Babyn Yar had ended, after a week of constant gunfire. A
woman from Kyiv described the slaughter, how she couldn't fathom
it, though she could hear it day by day, though she saw her neighbors being dragged from their houses, never to return.

Was Simcha brave, or foolhardy? He died anyway, broad-
shouldered, barrel-chested, bearded Simcha, trying to sneak behind
a guard to brain him with a hammer.

In 1942 in Kamin'-Kashyrs'kyi, a district commissar, part of the
Reichskommissariat visiting Liubeshiv, was wounded by a razor
blade wielded by a local dentist.

This is how resistance looked.

Mendel Blat steered the boat of Ratne, Y. Kanishter said, and Moshe
Honik, resettled in Buenos Aires, remembered Mendel Blat as an organizer of the charity fund of JOINT, awarding small business loans
a Joint Distribution Committee organizer of charity relief for Ratne.
Blat helped to found HaOved, a labor organization with headquarters in Warsaw, and when he organized the tradesmen of Ratne
into the Union of Tradesmen, he was the chief activist. As chief, he
helped to advocate on the behalf of a fellow tradesman whose goods
were unlawfully confiscated by Polish authorities. The taste of rep-
resentative government was sweet, if brief, and in 1928 Blat and others were elected to represent Jewish community councils among Poland's border districts.

The last word on Mendel Blat was Yisroel Chait's in the Ratne

Yizkor book. On July 17, 1941, a Judenrat was established in Ratne, and as in other towns and cities administered by the National Socialists, the members were chosen from the town's most respected citizens. Those chosen would then carry out Nazi orders and offer up colleagues, family, townspeople to satisfy forced labor and death quotas. Mendel Blat was among this chosen group of Judenrat. Chait said it was a disgrace to be a member of the Judenrat, prancing around like a ganef, licking Nazis' boots. The Judenrat wore white armbands in Ratne, their purpose "to create an air of importance. In truth, it adds to the disgrace of its owner in the eyes of the Jews who see it," Chait said. If Blat had refused to be a member of the Judenrat, he would have been executed on the spot. Instead, he chose to prolong his life and thus became despised. He might have been the first one killed when the shooting began in August 1942. Or perhaps he was forced to watch the annihilation of everyone else before he was shot on August 26. Perhaps he was thrown on top of his wife in the pit, still alive, only to have dirt shoveled over him.

Perhaps that wife was Esta Plat. Perhaps Mendel Blat tried to run away and was shot in the back. Or perhaps he did run and was stabbed in the woods by a town member avenging a brutality Mendel Blat committed during his long year of degradation.

Mendel Blat, traitor. Before they all died, Jewish men in Ratne crossed the street to avoid meeting Mendel Blat on the sidewalk.

People remember Mendel's wife as Sara, a woman too young to have been you, dear Esta. *Sara* is often a Hebrew placeholder for names forgotten, a Jane Doe of the Shoah. Was this the fate of Esta Plat in the minds of her fellow Ratners, to become a faceless Sara?

The Israeli choreographer and dancer Ohad Naharin tells a story in *Mr. Gaga* to explain why he dances. He is a twin, he said, and while he grew and thrived, his twin was uncoordinated, silent, and moody. The only time his brother would respond at all was when his grandmother danced for him. It seemed her dancing reached some otherwise untouchable part of him and made him happy and responsive, and he would laugh and clap while she twirled around the room.

One day, the family was on an outing, and on their way to Tel Aviv they had a car crash and Ohad Naharin's grandmother was killed. After her death, Ohad began to dance for his brother, taking his grandmother's place. In fact, during the documentary film, he tells the members of his dance company during practice one day to dance as though his life depended on the quality of their dancing. Because of the earlier anecdote, I believed he meant both literally and spiritually that his life does, in fact, hinge on dancing, his own dancing, and the dancing of the troupe performing his choreography.

The anecdote was delivered with such depth and sincerity I became a dervish bubbie, dancing out of love and desperation for my own grandchildren.

What does it mean, to dance for someone as though their life depended on it? I thought the story reflected on the grumpy archivist, sick to death of the unsuccessful ancestry searches he facilitated at the Central Archives for the History of the Jewish People. He knew full well what was in the archive and what wasn't, and like every visitor to the center, why. If he could send along a few photocopied sheets from a shtetl's salvaged wreckage, so much the better.

Later in the film, unprovoked, Naharin says that the story of his twin was fiction, that he didn't have a twin, though his grandmother did love to dance. He said he made up the story and has told it several times when people ask him for an explanation of why he loves to dance. I imagine that saying bluntly that his lifeblood is fueled by dancing didn't convey the truest sense of having to dance in order to live. Perhaps the constant task of illustrating the intangible got to him. After I watched the film, I got a sickening feeling about my photocopied sheets and examined them for the umpteenth time, each time relieved to see Mendel Blat's name. One of his donations is larger than the other, and one sum is smudged over with a blob of ink. Maybe his donations were just enough for three dozen notebooks for the young aspiring scholars who studied at the Great Yeshiva in Vilnius, and a box full of High Holy Days siddurs.

Mendel Blat, fellow Ratner, lived in an imaginative space much larger than the newly drained and cobbled streets of Ratne. I see him often during daydreams, boarding a train in Brest on his way to Vilnius, or traveling by train west to Warsaw, where he represented Ratne as the area began the long, slow, unsuccessful drive to unionize its workers. The pages that hold Mendel Blat's name transform, their records from a world not unlike my own, interlocked. Contributions go to local food banks and to assuage the wounds of countless injured and kidnapped people, murdered by men who refuse to put down arms and end their apocalyptic course.

Shoahtecture IV

A TOUR GUIDE THROUGH THE MAZE OF THE VALLEY of the Communities Memorial, Claudine sits in a simulacrum pit at Yad Vashem behind a window and hands out paper cups of ice water to those unaccustomed to the desert air. Outside the window of her office, parallel chisel marks on the bedrock columns that resemble both futuristic building blocks and wreckage remind some visitors of concentration camp prison clothes, they say. The chisel marks reminded me of prehistoric symbols in a cave counting ibex herds, wildebeest, and many gibbous moons. The rim of the simulacrum pit is planted with cascading, flowering shrubs, and though not the Hanging Gardens of Babylon, the green rim in the middle distance between the gravel pit and the infinite cerulean sky was being worked by bees.

Diminutive Claudine doesn't walk through a wall whose molecules she envisions rearranged, but with the right arrangement of Hebrew letters, she explains as she watches my husband and me drink the throat-numbing cold water she has offered us, she believes she will meet the Divine, because according to her, she has known Him. She lives in Jerusalem, she says, because Jerusalem "is where

God lives." She has been a tour guide for the Israeli Tourist Bureau for almost fifty years.

If no one had a question or felt obliged to wander through the 107 columns in the maze of the Valley of the Communities without a map, as I did not, Claudine would sit in silence all day long at the bottom of the canyon of chiseled names of all the cities, towns, and villages whose Jewish communities were destroyed in western and eastern Europe during World War II, the long death tally its only decoration. The lists are like an inventory of precious instruments destroyed in a symphony warehouse fire, among them the klezmer clarinet of Ratne, maybe yours, dear Esta.

A Parisian jeweler, Claudine's father fled to Palestine alone, so as not to draw the Vichy government's suspicion on his family's exit from Paris, Claudine said. He arranged passports for his wife and daughter, and for a guide to meet and lead them out of Paris. Claudine spoke quietly outside her glassed-in office, and once, a young armed guard came to check on her, and us. She sensed him approaching behind her and waved him away with a flit of her thin arm, the skin almost as veined and papery as Susha's and my mother's had become before their deaths.

Claudine's mother was wary of this plan, but as a devout Orthodox woman, she was accustomed to following the directions of her husband, yet she was also a woman about to travel alone during wartime without her mate, her staff, or her God, who seemed everywhere and nowhere. As surrogate protection, Claudine's mother held counterfeit documents for herself and her daughter. She would hand over her family's entire life savings to a stranger, a guide she had not met, and it turned out, she would never meet.

Claudine's mother taught Claudine before they fled that there is an art to stuffing the cavity of a doll, demonstrated on Colette, Claudine's favorite.

First, believe. Do not fixate on what would happen if SS agents found gemstones stuffed inside Colette the doll, for their mercy extended only to themselves. Likely they would flense and disembowel Claudine before her mother's eyes, before they blinded her. So, believe! Likely they would pull off dolly's limbs, then Claudine's, her mother's, dolly's plastic tongue, Claudine's, her mother's.

Even with so great a risk, Claudine believed she was a lucky one, *the* lucky one. It had to be that way, and for Claudine, it was. Every omen said so. Blue moons, Chełm, the magical Aleph orb, chthonic talismans, believe! To make things that much more mystical, or dangerous, Claudine could never, ever say Colette the doll was full of pearls, lockets, small diamonds that trickled down her hollow dolly neck when Claudine's mother removed the dolly's head. If you hanker for a happy-ending Shoah story, this is one, for the small Parisian family was reunited in Palestine along with Colette the doll, who lives permanently behind glass in a Yad Vashem exhibition of the toys children played with in their years of hiding or exile throughout the years of World War II.

Claudine flipped over the photocopied map of the pillars arranged in the Valley of the Communities and wrote a simple equation with a sharpened pencil for our gematria lesson.

"Consider hydrogen," she said. "One atom. Two hydrogens in water. Count that as a two, because hydrogen is one on the periodic chart: 1×2. Then, consider oxygen, number sixteen on the periodic chart. Assign sixteen, not a prime number: 4×4; 2×8; $2 \times 2 \times 2 \times 2$; $2 \times 2 \times 4$," she said as she wrote numbers precisely, as though with leaded type.

"Eighteen is the sum of two hydrogens and one oxygen, $2 + 16$, the molecular structure of water. There is little water where we are going, my friends," she said as she shook her finger like a scold.

"Consider *khes*, the eighth letter in the Hebrew alphabet, and consider *yod*, tenth. The word for "life" in Hebrew is *chai*, spelled *khes* and *yod*: $8 + 10 = 18$.

"There you have the proof," Claudine said, gentle but insistent, writing out the formula in her steady hand. But proof of what? That God and science are one? That Hebrew holds the key to life as water holds the key?

A young Polish man, one of my son Ezra's friends, studied the Kabbalah in London. I asked the friend if he'd heard of Ratne, but he hadn't. His father fled Warsaw with him in tow when Lech Wałęsa came to power, and he wasn't a student of more distant wars. "Head of the fox, tail of the lion," he asked me in a riddle, "which are you?"

"Head of the fox," I guessed, "fast, clever, cunning."

"No!" He shook his head, "No! Wrong choice! Foxes are cunning but hunted by hounds," prized for the tails women covet to wrap around their necks. Tail of the lion is the right response, so swift. It strikes, and bam, you're dead before regret sets in, knocked off your feet, neck snapped. Then, the pierce of teeth, blood lost, just like that. He dusted imaginary dirt from his hands and knees. Such nasty business, so much death.

"Riddle of my nightmares," Claudine had said as she handed me the map to make my way around the columns in the gravel pit to find the name *Ratne* chiseled in a stone.

Water. Life. Esta Plat?

Next to my mother's high school graduation photograph from 1939, she'd made corrections to her yearbook entry. She used pencil to correct the omission of her middle name. She chose blue ink to note her omitted club and honors affiliations, "Slide Rule, G.M.T.C., Spur," and she drew a rectangular box, in ink, around her name listed in the yearbook's index. Her photo appears on page thirty-nine. Her smile is close-lipped and noncommittal on her perfect, oval face. Elation or sorrow seem not to be the point; she looks prepared. Her head is slightly turned flirtatiously and she focuses left rather than straight at viewers. Her hair is tightly curled and lacquered into ringlets, and behind the curls at her forehead, she's pinned a little bow. A necklace with a delicate Star of David rests in the middle of her throat, at the *V* of her neckline a costume jewelry brooch she wished held diamonds. She signed the photograph my grandmother stored in the bottom of her hallway sideboard, "Love 'Babe' '39," one of her many nicknames.

Thirty-nine! Claudine might have said as she pressed her hands together. Three has heft, the essence of God, a triad of past, present, and future. Yes, Sad Angel, 1939 was the year Poland was invaded by the German army. As for nine, 3×3, my mother carried all three of her daughters to term, and let me tell you, we are pillars of stability. $3 + 9 = 12$. According to the gematria, it's a jackpot number: twelve tribes, twelve months in a Hebrew common year, the "completion of God's purpose."

In an invisible room in Yad Vashem, there is an archive from the Street of the Synagogue in Ratne that holds a glass doorknob from the house of Mendel Blat, who may or may not be the husband of Esta Plat. From the Street of the Synagogue, a jar of *varenye* preserved on a stovetop in 1941. *Varenye* was the fruit compote eastern European Jews put up and kept in their cupboards to nourish a family in hiding during pogroms. This varenye was simmered plums. Golda Meir called the nuclear program in Israel her varenye, thus varenye could also mean the Israeli nuclear site, Dimona.

At the nuclear site Dimona, an imaginary info-plaque recounts, Golda Meir's proxy enjoys Esta Plat's last jar of varenye, buried for more than seventy years on the Street of the Synagogue, a street bulldozed during Soviet administration of the town to lay the sewage line for an apartment building. Here is a map of where the tank tread, earth razed, Mendel Blat's house in grand collapse. Here is a flake of ash from the house William Lawitt and his father torched when they fled Ratne, because Lawitt said to his interviewer with the Shoah Foundation, he couldn't bear the thought that murderers would lie down in his house.

Another Ratne family left a jar of varenye on the kitchen table as they fled, hoping that whoever entered the house to ransack it would be satisfied with eating a jar of varenye. They were wrong, and what the archive holds is a broken table leg.

Here is a slingshot made with the tongue of a boy's shoe. The slingshot is a homemade weapon made famous in stories about King David. King David's identity is a mystery to some, but for a few shekels one can see his velvet-draped coffin in a former medieval abbey in Jerusalem's Old City.

When King David was a sassy boy, an info-plaque reminds, he used a slingshot to slay Goliath. The slingshot, more lethal than a razor blade, is an important symbol for hope against overwhelming odds. The archive offers a short video instruction.

Though grainy and erratic, the video suggests that to make a slingshot from the tongue of a shoe, the tongue should be double thick and long enough to hold a stone of at least two hundred grams. The stone needs to gather speed and spin for impact that makes a difference. "Difference" means hurt, maim, kill. But not too long a tongue; the stone can't get lodged or buried deep inside the tongue; it must release, propel.

To construct, eyeball the length of tongue. Leave enough tongue so that the shoe remains viable in flight.

Feel the heft of the tongue in your palm, the video's instructor says. *In better times, you might have carried marbles in Bright Angel's pouch, polished agates, tiger's eyes, pink quartz, or your little sister's baby teeth.*

Punch a hole through the tip of the tongue with an awl, the kind that cobblers use. Take care not to start the punch with a knife slit; the hole will grow too large. If no awl is available, or the cobbler has been murdered, use a nail, pound with hammer, shoe, another stone. Be inventive! Thread the hole with a strong, thin piece of shoelace, leather's best. Carry the slingshot under your shirt, on your belt.

One more hole, punch same, along the straight edge of one thickness of the tongue. Through this hole, thread the brown shoe-lace of the tongueless shoe. Take care that the shoelace is strong and that, when spun with a rock tucked in, the shoelace holds the tongue at a right angle from an invisible pole above the spinner's head. Take care when operating, for a slingshot's purpose is to con-cuss opponents, not oneself.

An ice pick is also on display. Someone found it in a gutter along a street called the Street of the Synagogue where Mendel Blat once lived. The archivist suggested that people carried ice picks for self-defense, and the ice pick is displayed in a block of ice that never melts.

The Pulse of Your
Quietest Word

M Y MOTHER-IN-LAW CALLED TO SAY THAT IN HER dream, her long-dead husband is still alive, living under an assumed name in Salt Lake City. Her husband perished in 1963, when his gull wing Stinson Reliant stalled in flight after taking off from the airfield in Massillon, Ohio. Someone had tossed a cigar in the fuel tank as a prank, and though others were dragged from the flames when the plane crashed into a hillside, her husband wasn't. My husband was not yet four years old.

In her dream, my mother-in-law sees her husband's photo and the caption underneath it with his name in a yearbook from the graduating class of the University of Utah. The picture is vivid and accurate, down to the smirk her husband affected in photographs similar to James Dean's. Her husband never completed his degree, never lived in Utah, but in her dream, she sets out on a quest to find him, to learn why he faked his death, his funeral, skipped town and abandoned her, leaving her to raise their son alone and repay his debts on her meager English teacher's salary. She soars to Salt Lake City on invisible, redemptive wings, as only dreamers or angels can, to leaf through the phone book at the Salt Lake City Public Library, where she finds a listing for him, living, not under an assumed name, but his own. Plain as day. She pokes the entry with her pointer finger to make sure it's not an illusion and the entry holds.

Despite what she thought she would feel, she is not overjoyed to find him alive; she is irked about the decades of deception, or rather, the decades during which she thought he was dead, not hiding from his former life. She dials the number listed in the phone book to chew him out. As she holds the receiver close to her ear, listening to the ringtone, she thinks better of speaking to him now and begins to hang up. After all, where, exactly, would she start if she tried to encapsulate her life without him, the life of her son, or her husband's parents, who never recovered from his accidental death.

Just as the receiver rests on the cradle of the black old-fashioned phone, she hears a huffed *H* starting to become "hello" before the line goes dead. The "he—" is a push of wind rather than a tone she thinks she recognizes, breath coming from the middle of his diaphragm, an intimate sound she has not heard for more than fifty years. For a day after, though she isn't given in her waking hours to speculations like those uncovered in her dream, she lets herself wonder if it could be true, if it could be possible that her husband faked his death to escape his life and start again in Salt Lake City. She checks online in the Salt Lake City phone book—no rogue husband—and in a few other cities where they had flown on larks together—same results. Feelings arose she hadn't counted on. What would she do if she had to care for an old man she hadn't known for fifty years?

So it is with the record of the life of Esta Plat, a woman lodged somewhere in dreamtime or plain view, hiding in a footnote, an index, an archive, a yet-to-be-unearthed and translated page, a name scribbled in pencil in Yiddish or Hebrew or English on the back of a photograph, a donor on a list of contributors who paid for the new prayer books at the Great Yeshiva in Vilnius, eastern Europe's once nexus of religious education. Esta Plat, the woman no one re-membered to name in the postwar hysteria of composing the ne-crology list for the destroyed community of Ratne, Esta Plat hid-ing like my father-in-law in my dreams, dear Esta living on a pretty street near Sacher Park in Jerusalem, where she picnics on a blue blanket on Saturday afternoons, eating cold boiled chicken and celery with a pinch of salt. See how she wiggles her ears while her great-grandchildren laugh and stand on their heads doing yoga in the park?

I sit at many desks from an infinity of archives in which Esta Plat does not appear. In the United States Holocaust Memorial Mu-seum Library, at the suggestion of research librarians, I view all the Shoah Foundation interviews with survivors from all over Volyn Province to see if they exhibited photographs during the interviews that just might be a photograph of Esta Plat, though I don't know what Esta Plat looked like. I knew the exercise was folly, but when our sons were small, my family frequented a small theater in Union, Oregon, to watch foreign films from Janus, the distributor of small-production, experimental films. Many programs included a short before the feature-length film, and one evening, the short was *Art Attack*, no credits, during which a man in a white hazmat suit, his eyes visible through a plastic shield on his hood, strolls trancelike through an art gallery hung with abstract paintings, his. I recog-nized the eyes, my cousin Elliott's, a man I'd met once at a New York wedding in 1964. I was certain of the eyes I'd seen more than thirty years before, and I was right.

If I could recognize my cousin's eyes through the plastic visor of a hazmat suit, could I recognize you, dear Esta, if I stood ankle deep in muck and clapped my hands? If only I knew where to look, would that be validation that you had lived as well as died? Would it ever be enough?

There is no photograph of Esta Plat amid Susha's other relatives, nothing in the group of six year olds standing in front of the Ratne

synagogue a generation before it was burned down, no eight, sixteen, or forty-year-old Esta horded as a keepsake by unimagined
friends I would not recognize either—a secret lover, her business
partner in the export of forest mushrooms, a woman she liked to
drink black tea with on Sunday afternoons. Even if her imagined
squarish face trying to force a smile had been among a stranger's
keepsake treasures, her chestnut-colored hair parted in the middle
and rolled like a Nez Percé princess wore her tresses, the display of
photographs during the interviews was always rushed, furtive, images in frames snatched from a wall or sideboard, an addendum to
the compilation of nightmares others had the foresight to preserve.

The Mount of Olives filled the close horizon to the south, below
the Jerusalem skyline sere brown hills and haze, faded gray-green
cypress trees. A fence separated the men's section of the Kotel, the
Western Wall, from the women's section, in addition to the larger
fence separating off the close distance from the Kotel to the middle
of the plaza. A large, raised wooden platform for bar and bat mitzvah celebration guests, along with speakers and floodlights, created
a mesh and timber hodgepodge between the ramshackle platform
and the steps leading up from the plaza made broad enough for military vehicles to amass. Formal Sabbath services had ended, much
of the crowd dispersed. The din in the plaza muted to a murmur
pierced by singular yelps of ecstasy and two men shouting at each
other while poking each other's chests as they stood in the men's
section of the Kotel.

I knew a jeweler who thought that with enough concentration,
he could put his fist through a brick wall. He'd heard a lecture by
a physicist whose topic was flux and matter, the rearrangement of
molecules, with a dash of mind control thrown in. The jeweler, well
known for his picture-jasper pendants, smoked a lot of weed long after he'd blown a fuse on LSD. "If one willed matter to reconfigure,"
he'd said, one could punch a hole through anything. The jeweler

had tried it, unsuccessfully, a few times, but he said he hadn't "committed" to the experiment with a full-on punch, because he said if he broke his hand, he couldn't work, and if he couldn't work, he couldn't pay child support. The jeweler said you could do the same with your entire body, but he hadn't tried that yet.

If I remained outside the perimeter of the Kotel, I could maintain the pure distance of my cynic's gaze. I focused on a woman I'd seen earlier in the morning buying dried apricots from a vendor who'd set up his table at the base of a statue of King David strumming on his lyre near the Dormition Abbey. She walked backward on tiptoe from the Kotel, graceful as a boxer in the gym, followed by a trickle of other women, all of them stepping gingerly with spiked heels among the cobbles, their rapture erased by the more imminent task of exiting the enclosure without tripping, breaking a heel in the cobbles' cracks, gracelessly ruining the moment of devotion even as they honored the tradition of holy protocol.

They'd done it, though, hadn't they?

They'd taken the steps forward to the sacred wall; they'd believed in the possibility of rearranging molecules; they'd placed their hands on the stones. And if I followed suit, would I be suddenly transformed, relieved, infused with gratitude, bathed in revelation? Would I hear the loudspeaker proclaim with the accent of a thousand languages the name of Esta Plat?

I recalled watching my children learn to dive, their hesitation on the edge of the springy board, their peer into the deep below, me counting the seconds until their plastered hair atop their crowns popped above the surface of the water, their foreheads, eyes and noses, mouths, and thrashing, skinny arms that followed. Faith folded into physics, buoyancy in water. I'd done the dives, for many years devout during Saturday reflections, humbled, waiting for a sign from God that never came.

I waited in the square for the blare of angelic trumpets but heard only a bullhorn announcing the time of the next tour through the

Old City's narrow streets. I could, I thought, simply touch the wall as though passing a baton to another runner in a relay and turn away.

My steps smaller than the length of my feet, I minced past the empty white plastic chairs lined up row by row in the women's section, hesitated behind two dozen women praying, standing, swaying, stroking the stones of the wall like a pelt. I stopped an arm's length short, the height of the Kotel casting a cool shadow onto the shoulders of many praying women. Green tendrils of thorny capers curled from the chinks out of reach, and swallows darted through labyrinths of air above our heads. Notes of devotion folded and stuffed in the Kotel's lower cracks fluttered like the gills of deep-sea fish. A note stuffed in a crack fell at the feet of a woman wearing a bright green T-shirt that said "Lagos" on the back. As she bent to pick up the note, her right hand covered the large wooden crucifix dangling from a leather strip around her neck. She smoothed the surface of the note and placed it in a crack above her head without reading it. After she left, a gray dove knocked the note out of the wall again.

A small space adjacent to the Kotel opened in front of me as a woman to my right, forehead touching the wall, straightened her back and, sensing my presence, took a step to the right so that I could move beside her. She raised her head. A red oval flushed on her forehead from the pressure of her skull against the stone, the only color in the otherwise gray hues of her long-sleeved blouse and skirt and skin. The tremor in her outstretched hands relaxed as she drew her Hebrew prayer book closer to her chest. Her gaze ventured neither right nor left, locked on the ocher-colored block in front of her, its smooth surface polished by many hands. So many delicate women's hands, the stones' surfaces rubbed by fingertips greasy with the body's oils—leaf and petal lotions, saffron, mint, lemon, figs—supplicants' hands. Her exhale was like a sleeping child's. I held my breath as if to hear the final vibration of an echo.

The woman to my left navigated the last few steps to the wall on tiptoe, her tight black skirt rustling softly as she moved. She placed her right palm flat against the wall and with her left lifted the small gold crucifix around her neck to her red lips and held it there. Her sunglasses hid her eyes, her cheeks streaked with damp mascara. The three of us shifted together, dancers in that spot. The woman to my left watched as I bent to pick up a folded note lying at my feet. The brittle white paper was too thick for the cracks between the lower blocks. If I opened the note and refolded it, the note might tear, but it might also have a better chance of remaining in a chink, until the notes grew so plentiful attendants removed them all and buried them in a consecrated cemetery nearby in anticipation of another raft of notes. At least the note in my hand wouldn't fall out of the crack and get trampled again so soon.

I turned back the note's first fold.

"Señora!" the woman standing next to me whispered with caution. "No!" She pointed to the note in my hand and shook her finger.

I could have explained that I wasn't going to read the note, just refold it thinner, but the only sound around us was our breathing and hands softly brushing tears from our cheeks. A thigh thudded against a plastic chair. A purse clasp caught, a pen clicked shut, a turning page rustled in the prayer book held next to me. The woman on my right began to hum the melody of a prayer I thought I recognized. The note I'd picked up felt hot between my fingers. I pressed down the folded edge as best I could to make it fit more snugly in a crack I thought was deeper than the others. If a note of mine had fallen to the ground and ended up a laminated good-luck charm, a relic from the Holy Land a woman secreted away from the Kotel, would I object? And if she carted it around in her handbag along with an extra N95 facemask for the next pandemic or drought-induced fire, who was I to tell her she was wrong to eavesdrop on a one-way correspondence with God?

Dear Esta, I imagined myself writing on a tiny slip of paper to slide into a space between two Kotel stones, *how pliable a stone feels, your name murmuring through my fingertips.*

I stretched my fingers flat, my palms, my life lines merging with every other woman's hands as I stepped through a portal into a brief and perfect silence. I realized something the jeweler hadn't, that it wasn't a brutish punch that would reveal a secret passageway through solid matter. So much rubbing and caressing of these fortress stones had accelerated the erosion that would rearrange the molecules enough to open up a keyhole to someone else's bliss. Even now, when I look at the palms of my outstretched hands, and after a thousand washings, I see the Kotel's molecules refracted in a symmetry like hope. It smells citrusy, like the *etrog* passed around on Sukkot.

A searing edge of sun lanced the periphery of my sight. Light split into all the rainbow's bands. Sighted. Blinded. My palms leaned into stone as a white gauze veil descended from beyond the Kotel, above it, draped my head and wrapped softly over my shoulders and my arms, waist, hips, legs, the minute gaps of the cloth's loose weave filled with time and timelessness.

Whispers spilled from all the women's lips, scented with their perfumes—sandalwood, forget-me-not, orange blossoms, frangipani. We women, that congress, these lives. The Kotel inhaled and exhaled without gills, lungs, stomata, each breath all our breaths, together, each entreaty blended. In what language were the answers uttered, and at what timbre?

Codices

T HE ALEPPO CODEX, ALSO CALLED THE CROWN, IS the oldest complete canonical text of the Hebrew Bible, the Tanakh—Five Books of Moses, Prophets, Writings. Rescued and housed in Aleppo, Syria, for generations after Crusaders stole it in 1099 during the sacking of Jerusalem, it is the codex Maimonides traveled from Spain to Egypt to consult in the twelfth century, when he wrote the Mishneh Torah. Because many factions of Haredi believe the Aleppo Codex contains Kabbalistic codes and numeric, secret messages about the pathway to the Divine hidden in its leaves, the manuscript, to protect it, was imbued with gruesome curses for all potential thieves, and prohibitions—no buying or selling of the leaves, no dismantling of the Crown for any reason, no viewing of its contents with an impure heart. It is the ultimate *Pinkas* book, a map of the mindset of God.

The partial Aleppo Codex is locked in a vault at the Israel Museum. Several leaves are missing, roughly 40 percent of the manuscript, though when the Crown was housed in a vault in the Syrian Great Synagogue in the old Jewish section of Aleppo, it was extant. Fishy details surround the clandestine removal of the Crown after an arson attack on the Aleppo Great Synagogue in 1947, one of many casualties after the riot that ensued against Jews in Aleppo when the U.N. General Assembly voted to establish the country of Israel.

For ten years after the fire, members of the Aleppo Jewish community closest to the synagogue's administration did not contradict the belief that the Crown had been destroyed, though "scattered pages," Ronen Bergman reported in the *New York Times Magazine*, were saved by Asher Baghdadi and his son after the fire.

Rumors about the destruction of the manuscript persisted, while antiquities dealers privately searched for clues to help them locate supposedly hidden leaves. There are scores of devout and innocent and pure of heart who seek to uncover the pathway to the Divine, and others who seek lucre's path from the sale of sacred manuscripts, objects, and ephemera. The Mossad, the Syrian Intelligence Agency, and Israel's Jewish Agency were all looking for the Crown.

What is gained by perpetrating fiction over truth is time, hoping for government stabilization, dominance of one branch of Judaism or another, an ebbing of the anti-Semitic tide that swept the region after the establishment of Israel. Bargaining with *ruhot* (demons) is risky business, but that is what happened when the Aleppo Codex was hidden in Aleppo after the great synagogue fire of 1947, according to Matti Friedman in his extensive study, *The Aleppo Codex*, secreted out of Syria to Turkey, and delivered to Jerusalem in 1957 to the Ben-Zvi Institute, complete with a request to the rabbinate from then-president Yitzhak Ben-Zvi to annul the curses associated with the Aleppo Codex's secret transfer to Jerusalem.

Uncharacteristic of a professional archive claiming to be *the* archive for the written history of Judaism, when the Crown was delivered to the chief curator at the institute, he did not record basic archival information about the receipt of the codex—condition of the leaves, number of leaves present in the manuscript, other pertinent information about the size, shape, and contents of the codex.

Several sources tell two similar stories about bar mitzvah boys who, its outer gates akimbo, walked into the smoldering ruin of the Great Synagogue of Aleppo in 1947. Leon Tawil, fifteen at the time, found a great heap of parchment more than a yard high. Tawil grabbed a fragment and ran with it, later showed it to his father, who judged it to be the concluding leaf from the Crown's second book of Chronicles, "and let him go up" (2 Chronicles 36:26–27). Leon Tawil and his family immigrated to Brooklyn and eventually the fragment was passed to his niece, who sent it to the Ben-Zvi Institute in the 1980s. The proof of the leaf heartened others to rekindle the theory that the missing leaves had been shuffled and appropriated among members of the Aleppo Jewish community, especially since proof otherwise, in the form of fifty-year sealed rabbinical court proceedings, outlined the claim from Aleppo Jews that the Crown had been stolen from them by agents of the Ben-Zvi Institute.

Once the seal's statute of limitations had expired, Friedman and Bergman posited the institute's internal theft of the leaves. They concluded that the London-based antiquities expert now possessing the missing leaves of the Crown, curses aside, cannot sell them in his lifetime, given the continued zealous hunt for them and the claim by Aleppo's now-scattered Jewish community that they were stolen.

My husband and I spent an alternately spirited and dispiriting afternoon at the Israel Museum marveling at what was saved, tantalized by relics from Herod's empire, the cerulean blue tiles from his bath, a nautical rope of hemp, an anchor from a ship that plied the Mediterranean's waters to fetch the vessels of the Spanish figs and anchovies Herod loved to eat, all objects standing testament to the majesty of his rule. Even Herod's hygiene rag would have been more important than a leaf from Ratne's *Pinkas* book with Esta's name. I smarted from humiliation for daring to look for a scrap of paper that recorded something about the life of so common a Polack as Esta Plat.

How many more curses are there to lift from the charred ink of Ratne's Codex? How much more blood sacrifice?

The Shrine of the Book, adjunct of the Israel Museum, houses the leaves of the Aleppo Codex in a vault less visible than the vault in Mainz where the Gutenberg Bible is on display. Beginning in 2012, another fragment of the Crown a little larger than a business card, once laminated and carried in Samuel Sabbagh's back pocket, was mounted on display behind bulletproof glass. Soothingly lit, its silent power seduces like a night-blooming cereus.

Curses upon those who defile the Crown!

Like the plotline in Leon Tawil's story, Sabbagh recalled going to the Great Synagogue after the fire, found a fragment of parchment on the floor, and according to Friedman, "took it." He didn't explain how he knew the fragment was from the Crown; the synagogue's library housed hundreds of sacred texts as well as the Crown. He just knew, he claimed.

Sabbagh also immigrated to Aleppo's diasporic community in Brooklyn, and he believed the fragment had the power to help him survive open-heart surgery. Though he was contacted in 1987 by Michael Glatzer to return the fragment, and again in 1988 by Menahem Ben-Sasson, until his death, Sabbagh kept the fragment from the book of Exodus describing the plagues of blood and frogs in his back pocket.

In Robert Alter's translation of the book of Exodus, Moses, "uncircumcised of lips" (Exodus 6:30) and his brother, Aaron, turn the Nile to blood, every drop of water, "rivers, canals, ponds, and pools," even the household vessels holding river water for drinking and cooking. Fish gills filled with blood, ibises and cranes with blood-filled fish, so much blood the air was filled with the smell of melting copper. When blood didn't prove a convincing enough demonstration of God's serious intent to free the Israelites from bondage to Egyptians, so the story goes, Moses and his brother waved a magic staff and with it cursed the land of Egypt with frogs, so many slimy amphibians hopping out of rivers, and not the juicy frog legs my aunt TT liked to eat during Sunday brunch at Mount Vernon, a dining club in the foothills west of Denver.

Sabbagh's heirs returned the fragment from the Crown's book of Exodus to the museum, who corroborated its authenticity. How about that, dear Esta? A scrap of paper! What a lucky grab.

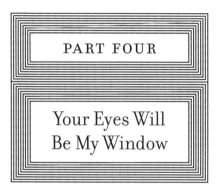

PART FOUR

Your Eyes Will
Be My Window

Your Eyes Will
Be My Window

NADINE ERTUGRUL WAS MURDERED SOMETIME between Monday, October 12 and October 20, 2015, in Eglosheim, a small German village that borders Ludwigsburg. Ertugrul was tall and broad shouldered, strong, athletic, a photogenic, thirty-six-year-old ethnic German woman with long, bleached-blond hair. Until the time of her murder, she worked in the Porsche factory in Stuttgart. She had two daughters, an estranged husband, and many friends in the communities of Eglosheim and Ludwigsburg.

The night she disappeared, Nadine E., as the press began to call her, was wearing black jogging tights, a black camisole, and a yellow tank top that police divers searched for on the muddy bottom of nearby Monrepos Lake. Newspaper articles didn't divulge details that would suggest a struggle or kidnapping, but Nadine Ertugrul was sturdy and vital, according to people who knew her, an avid jogger, no stranger to the rigors of hard work. She was, by many accounts, a woman who could take care of herself. Her estranged husband was questioned by the police and was not at first a suspect. The apartment of her new boyfriend was searched, but by the end of December 2015, he was no longer considered a person of interest in the crime. By the time my husband and I arrived after New Year's Day in 2016 to work with Peter Dines at the Ludwigsburg University of Education, the police called the case "cold."

Before Nadine E.'s murder, students at the university joked that nothing out of the ordinary happens in Ludwigsburg, a town of roughly eighty-eight thousand people about twelve kilometers north of Stuttgart. Even less happens, they said, in Eglosheim, a working-class village of Turks, Croats, Kosovars, Albanians, Syrians, and African asylum seekers. Before Nadine E.'s murder, students and staff assured me when I was in Ludwigsburg teaching alone that women could move about freely at night without fear of assault or harassment, but now they feel afraid. If Nadine E. could take care of herself, is murder the result of a woman taking care? Does her age matter? The color of her skin? Her creed? Her country of origin?

On October 12, 2015, at 8:30 p.m., Nadine Ertugrul left the Eglosheim apartment she shared with her mother, her estranged husband, Ramazan, and two young daughters. She drove to the Lidl grocery outlet store across from the Ludwigsburg University campus on Reuteallee to buy snacks. Nadine E. parked and locked her car on Eduard Spranger Street across Reuteallee, rather than in the Lidl lot, or at least that is where her car was found. At 9:30 p.m. on October 12 her cell phone logged a call, but that record is the only detail the newspaper revealed. Her cell phone was not found in the car or near her body. According to Lidl clerks, Nadine E. had "shopped a bit." She did not return home on the twelfth, after a trip that should have taken less than fifteen minutes. According to the *Bietigheimer Zeitung*, a small newspaper in a nearby town, on October 16 her mother notified the police that Nadine E. was missing, and on October 20, her nude body was discovered a few blocks away from the Lidl grocery outlet, in a ditch between a bramble patch and a berm that rises to support the train tracks between

Ludwigsburg and Marbach. Nadine E.'s neck and throat had "massive cuts," the first report said, and it was assumed that the wounds caused her death. The article by Tim Höhn on October 23 published on the *Stuttgarter Nachrichten* website mentioned, in the headline, only that Nadine E.'s autopsy revealed no sex crimes had been perpetrated on her body.

Nadine E.'s body was found directly across the street from the university guest apartment at Reuteallee 48, where my husband and I have sometimes stayed while in residence at the university. During the autumn and early winter of 2014, I lived there alone, while directing a seminar and researching two Holocaust memorial projects in Ludwigsburg, the Stolpersteine Initiative project and the redesign of the memorial for the Ludwigsburg synagogue burned to the ground during the Kristallnacht pogrom in November 1938.

The apartment's isolation at the end of a dark cul-de-sac made it impossible to sleep without dread, rational or not, even in quiet Ludwigsburg. Night on Reuteallee fell like a pall. Many nights I gazed into the dark, watching for the last passenger train to Marbach at 11:54 p.m., hungry for a view of the comfortable discomfort of passengers, their brown, black, or blond hair atop featureless faces, necks bent as they read papers, iPhones, or books. Occasionally, a passenger turned to glance my way, an anonymous other speeding away even as she approached. I longed to be among them, but when the train stopped at its destination, would I be one of those women who people remarked could take care of herself, wondering during each step if it were safe to walk alone in the dark? Instead, I kept on, inhabiting daytime with the efficiency of manageable expectations, nighttime in a parallel universe of fear.

For several days in October 2014, during which the university was closed, the front door to the guest apartment at Reuteallee 48 dislodged and would not lock. I tied it shut with an electrical cord I anchored to the handrail leading up a narrow stairwell to the apartment. The night my roommates and I were raped many years before, a woman at another crime scene a few blocks away had been bound with a similar cord, that one yellow, and her hair set on fire after her assailant broke into her apartment and raped her.

The lockless door with its futile, knotted cord magnified a sense of uncontrollable terror I have spent a lifetime trying to dissipate, and darkness on Reuteallee formed a noose around my heart. For weeks afterward, a panic loop that began long ago with my mother's senseless beatings combined with her remarks that I was somehow careless and therefore responsible for being raped played a death fugue in my head. When I learned that Nadine E.'s body had been found across the street, *of course* was my first response. That's what's doled a woman taking care. Even on Reuteallee, a nondescript, mostly peaceful street in a quiet, baroque-themed town, violence is real. Violence against women is real. The perpetual war against women is real.

Nadine E.'s body was obscured by a dense thicket of blackberry brambles, which her murderer, or the person who dumped her corpse, would have had to part and push through in order to drop her in the ditch. He must have clutched her body tightly, cradled in his arms, pressing her bare breasts against his chest to use her like a shield against the wall of thorns, to keep his shirt from tearing.

Some people gossiped that Nadine E.'s death had the trappings of an honor killing, as death contracts were called, perpetrated by a member of her husband's family or acquaintances of the family from her husband's ancestral Turkish home, who may or may not have been known to her husband or Nadine E. The couple was going to divorce, amenably, it seemed, according to thirdhand information, and her husband was on good terms with his mother-in-law and wanted to remain close to his two daughters. Nadine E. was in a new relationship, with a man known to her husband. Likely, people said, the murderer or murderers slipped away to another part of Germany, or to another country in the EU, perhaps back to Turkey, perhaps to the town from which some said the edict to murder Nadine E. arose.

Worldwide, we know that women die in the heat of passion; we know women are murdered during fits of mindless jealousy. Women disappear in the throes of war, as they are disappearing now in Ukraine, their bodies defiled. In another time, women were bad luck on boats and sometimes disappeared at sea. In Montana, native women disappear from reservations, rest stops, school and market parking lots. Sometimes they freeze to death by the side of the road, but more often rape and murder are used as weapons not only against them but against the communities and cultures in which they live. Daughters are left distraught and orphaned, and sons grow up with their own sense of justice and trajectory of vengeance.

According to the World Health Organization, at least 38 percent of all of the world's women and girls have been assaulted, sexually and/or physically, by people they know: lovers, relatives, friends—1,330,000,000 women and girls, more than three times the entire population of the United States. Many perpetrators remain at large, unpunished. All of us know of a woman or girl who lives not only in the shadow of violence but with the knowledge that at any time, the private sanctuary of a female body can be stripped of rights, battered, kicked, raped, destroyed. Seemingly benign environments—IKEA-furnished apartments, public streets, office parties—and gestures encountered throughout the day—an almost leer justified as good fun, a hand that lingers too long just above the buttocks, catcalls, vulgar taunts, overt demands for sex—trigger wariness, caution, debilitating fear.

Should we wonder who among our acquaintances will assault or rape us, and who will slay us? Would the wondering make us safer or staunch the dread? Should we embrace the fear: "Take back the night," as protesters chanted euphemistically at my university forty years ago, angry young women too embarrassed to say the word *rape* in public spaces, as I still am? Could a shrine or memorial, with its day-by-day reminder, begin to assuage our grief and help us to celebrate the lives of women taking care?

Reporter Sniegè Balčiūnaitė photographed a rape protest in Vilnius, Lithuania, on April 19, 2022, women responding in solidarity to the rapes of women and girls in Ukraine by Russian troops. The young women in the photo are much bolder than protesters were as we held our tidy, handwritten signs and pretended all we wanted was to stroll alone at night unmolested on our college campus.

The photo from Vilnius shows a line of young women with bags over their heads, hands tied behind their backs, mock prisoners of rage. They stand in front of the Russian Embassy in Vilnius with coats on, in white underpants, barelegged. Fake blood is smeared on their legs, their thighs, their shoes, on the outside of their underpants by their vulvas, anuses, buttocks. The photo makes me ask—did not representing rape in this vivid, honest way make us complicit in the silencing of such a massive crime? Where is the memorial for crimes against women?

The makeshift shrine erected at the site of the discovery of Nadine Ertugrul's body formed immediately after the white crime scene tent was removed by the police in October. In January 2016, when my husband and I returned to live in the apartment on Reuteallee together, a sea of red votive candles spread out at the edge of the ditch, the site shorn of its bramble canes like the tresses from the hair of a shamed woman accused of consorting with the enemy. The votive candles were the ubiquitous ones sold at Lidl for All Saints Day, red-glass cylinders encasing long-burning candles, the cylinders topped with peaked gold metal caps to prevent the candle flames from being extinguished in the rain.

Two and a half months after Nadine E.'s corpse was found, her shrine included two bouquets of flowers wrapped in purple tissue paper, potted heather, potted sedum that Germans often plant atop the cemetery plots of their deceased beloveds. A short wooden cross bore the name *Nadine* on the left side of the patibulum and the word *warum* (why) on the right, yellow and blue ribbons wound around the stipes of the cross, and at the base her daughters' photos, next to the photos a poem laminated in plastic. One day there was a necklace of silver beads wound around the stipes, but the day after, the necklace had slipped to the ground. Though I never witnessed people bending to light candles, every night the flames in the red candles flickered around the cross that bore Nadine E.'s name. If there were only a few white flames, my spirits flagged, though I never went out after dark to check the candles or the wicks or contribute a freshly lit votive to Nadine E.'s shrine.

Jochen Faber, who dubbed the guest apartment at Reuteallee 48 "cheerless and Soviet," was among the first to launch the Stolpersteine Initiative Group in Ludwigsburg, after his daughter asked him one evening what had happened in Ludwigsburg during World War II.

Conceived by Cologne artist Gunter Demnig in 1992, a stumble stone is a humble marker of the murdered during World War II, a small cobblestone ten by ten centimeters inlaid among other cobbles on the sidewalk in front of the last known residence of the deceased. The core of the marker is stone, the face bronze. The inscription on bronze bears the name of the deceased, maiden name if applicable, date of birth, birthplace, date of arrest, deportation site, death site, cause of death, date of death. The dull sheen on the bronze markers on any European street arrests the eye and reminds casual pedestrians not only of the town's vanished citizens but of its invisible history still living all around them.

Though scholars of the period and the area could easily answer Faber's daughter, produce a detailed list of Ludwigsburg citizens deported, murdered, or disappeared in abattoirs masked as euthanizing hospitals for mentally and physically challenged children and adults, and though copious files had been compiled and stored

since 1958 at the Central Office of the State Justice Administrations
for the Investigation of National Socialist Crimes, housed in Ludwigsburg, the information the files contained about crimes committed not only against the citizens of Ludwigsburg but throughout all the territory administered by the National Socialist regime
during World War II was not shared with the public at large. As a
father, a journalist, a documentarian, the son of a minister, and a
citizen of Ludwigsburg, Faber began the research that would lead
to public discussions, films, published biographies, and the installation of stumble stones marking the homes of several of Ludwigsburg's vanished citizens.

Demnig installs every stone, over 70,000 now, and counting. He
removes a section of asphalt, cement, or cobblestone in front of a
threshold on a quiet or busy European or Scandinavian street, in
front of the home of a vanished child or adult. The section of sidewalk is replaced with a stumble stone, reset less than a centimeter
above the surface of the surrounding sidewalk, so that pedestrians
will feel a slight obstruction on the tips of their toes or the balls of
their feet as they step on the uneven surface. Demnig's intentional
outcome is to elicit a pause by passersby, a glance down, a discovery
of a brief text on a bronze plaque set into the sidewalk noting the
lingering presence of one long-thought disappeared.

I've watched pedestrians in Ludwigsburg bend to read and photograph the stumble stones for Harry Grenville's father, mother,
and grandmother, Jakob and Klara Greilsamer and Sara Ottenheimer, installed in the sidewalk in front of Harry's childhood
home in Ludwigsburg. I have also watched pedestrians step on or
roll baby strollers over the bronze surfaces without so much as a
glance down, and once I watched from across the street of Harry's childhood home as a young man tossed the uneaten remainder
of his *döner* kebab on the sidewalk over Jakob and Klara's stones,
smearing the bronze with a blob of yogurt and shredded purple
cabbage. The stumble stone for the Bosch factory labor organizer

Oskar Mannheim, a devout Catholic, is set in front of an apartment block across the street from the Ludwigsburg Palace, close to the curb rather than the threshold of the apartment in which Mannheim last lived. In November 2014 I passed Mannheim's stumble stone on my way to a benefit concert to raise money for the Stolpersteine Initiative Group, a car's right front tire parked over the stone to its edge.

The disregard stings, but the absence of history, other than the preservation of the quaint lodgings of aristocrats, stings more. When I step near stumble stones, they make my feet ache.

Colleagues in Jochen Faber's office knew of Nadine Ertugrul. Nadine E. is still an individual, a unique, recognizable woman out of the world's 1.33 billion women and girls who have been assaulted, raped, and/or murdered. Her singular death sent ripples of upset through the community.

Seeing Nadine E.'s shrine by day and the red candles glowing night after night, I found myself inured to the sites of the stumble stones I customarily passed. Nadine E.'s shrine was newer, fresher, more spontaneous, her death closer. Her body was found across the street from an apartment in which I slept. The individuals marked with stumble stones, culled from the loss of so many, had merged into the legion of the dead, suspended in the process of continuous identification and erasure. The currency of so many stumble stones fades. The memory of those who perished over seventy years ago during World War II is crowded by the casualties of newer wars, foreign wars, domestic wars, our wars, the wars against us, the wars against women's bodies, the wars we fight against one another with weapons that can fire a bullet every four seconds. And now, Nadine Ertugrul is the unwitting victim in an investigation grown "cold."

Is it human suffering we wish to memorialize, the fundamental precept of human dignity, the world's Nadines? What would you say, dear Esta? Do the dead ache to be remembered, or do the living bear the burden of this sorrow?

———————

Thick, heavy snowflakes fell as my husband and I arrived just before dusk on a recent trip to Berlin, a city of shrines, memorials, and walls both visible and imagined. The gritty sidewalks blunted the ice from the previous storm, and the next storm was just picking up momentum, its large, wet, wind-driven flakes dissipating before they stuck to the winding paths and soggy loam in the Tiergarten where we were walking.

The city around the park was still before Friday rush hour, Straße des 17. Juni mostly deserted. A hallucinogenic string of colored ribbons swirled around my burning eyes, my feet rubbery, flapping as though I were trying to clomp along the path in swim fins wrapped in spurs. The slap of tires on pavement was muffled by the beating of my heart, my breath obstructed with what seemed a wad of suffocating gauze. My forehead burned with fever. I didn't know it then, but I had just said my last goodbye to Christoph Brudi, who died not long after.

I had wanted a stroll to conjure something other than murder and the aftermath of war, indulge in a frivolous fantasy of the Belle Epoque, the twentieth century's first world war not yet begun, its horrors and the horrors of the next war and the next and the next unknown as we strolled on the quiet, winding path. If a pair of spats had dropped down from the sky, I would have put them on. I wanted the tall, sprawling, leafless oaks that had been replanted to remain untouched for generations forward, recalling that all of the mature trees in the Tiergarten were cut for firewood during the winters between 1940 and 1942.

But why this turn away? Why the longing for this kind of respite? Wasn't the ruse of the Belle Epoque part of the deadly stall on addressing the ills of modernity? Spats, no less; how absurd is that! Is calm even possible after crawling underneath Satan's hairy balls?

Two foxes darted across the path near an empty food concession and disappeared into the small opening between shrubs and the edge of a chain-link fence. Their red, bushy tails erect behind them, they ran as foxes often run, always sensing danger, always looking for cover and an avenue of escape. Except for them and us, the forest park was deserted. Violence, in the city that commemorates violence on a massive scale, seemed remote, even as protesters prepared to march for agricultural reform near the Reichstag the next morning.

Coming and going from the Tiergarten, we circled the Victory Column with its gilded angel perched on top. The angel seems to grace the park, spear in one hand, laurel wreath in the other, welcoming all of those who behold her. I mistook her meaning; the angel was first a symbol not of peace but of victory for the empire of Wilhelm I after the Franco-Prussian War. More accurate for depicting the aftermath of war would have been a blob of red paint splattered on the folds of her stone gown cloaking her genitalia, two roses of blood surrogate for her mutilated breasts.

But this angel is not the angel commemorating the female victims of pogroms, nor does she stand to remind the world of how women are raped, mutilated, murdered day by day. The angel atop the Victory Column was moved by Hitler's chief architect, Albert Speer, to serve as sentry for the future imagined capitol of Germania, the sad angel proclaiming the victory of fascism. How important it must have seemed that the robust statue emanate virginity and strength.

During the Cold War, the angel atop the Victory Column became a symbol of democracy in West Berlin, mocking the German Democratic Republic, and now, more than thirty years after Germany's reunification, in yet another transformation of meaning, Berliners called the angel "Goldelse," the angel of gay pride.

In Berlin I got to counting not memorials but armed guards, police, and children begging. At the door to the Leo Baeck Institute a half-block away from the Neue Synagoge Berlin, a policeman standing guard. At the door to the synagogue, with its shrine of empty space where the Ark of the Covenant once stood, three policemen, security guards, and metal detectors before one could enter the synagogue through steel doors. Ditto security at the Memorial to the Murdered Jews of Europe and the Holocaust Museum.

There is a mindfulness about all the memorials to murdered Jews in Germany, bombed and burned-out synagogues, the needless casualties of war, a mindfulness that tries to approach the meaning of so much loss and destruction. In every instance, history and the resurgence of nationalist dictators across the world make the gesture an incomplete trap that has no exit. In Berlin, the backdrop to so much hand-wringing shame is the massive column work around and on the Brandenburg Gate, which tries to replicate the grandeur and folly of ancient Rome. The mythology of antiquity is stifling, but I wonder what will be left of the Sony Building or the new Potsdamer Platz dome constructed with so much glass.

Outside the stelae labyrinth of the Memorial to the Murdered Jews of Europe, its cement monoliths reminding of gravestones and crematoria stacks, pedestrians on their way elsewhere streamed by on the street with not so much as a glance at the memorial. Inside the cockeyed maze, I saw a sparrow picking at crumbs of someone's potato chips munched during a walk through the narrow, symbolic, land beyond the living. A child sat leaning her back against a stele in the center of the maze. Her two front teeth missing, she parted her lips shyly, as though to speak. Instead, she handed me a note that said, "I speak a little English. My brother needs a coat."

We saw the girl the next day begging in front of the Neue Wache memorial, whose bronze sculpture was inspired by Kathë Kollwitz's *Mother with Her Dead Son*, a depiction of an adult child dead and draped in the lap of his grieving mother. She is whole and strong, as women are expected to be, her heavy, milky breasts and heaving chest clothed in gentle metal folds, no red paint splattered on her breasts to suggest a Cossack had maimed her before he slit her throat. To face the truth, memorials enshrine spectators' mincing steps during their museum crawls, affecting varying levels of piety and disregard. Memorials enshrine the needy beggar girl and whoever she fled her country with, her cousins, her mother; children of many countries reduced to rags and bones. Can the grieving bronze woman holding her dead son hold all the war dead of all wars, all the victims of dictators' vindictive murders?

Can you, dear Esta?

People walking around the *Pietà*-inspired statue in the Neue Wache memorial taking photos seemed obedient in their notice of war and death, numbed yet amplified by the memorial's invisible force that tried to capture how death feels to the living.

How does death feel to the living? Pain rises up and up, culminating in a dome with an opening like a dilated cervix. Then, no heaven, no happy peal of birth. Then, nothing.

On our last evening in Berlin, my husband and I ate dinner at an Iranian restaurant close to our hotel. While we were waiting for our meal, a little girl in a red dress with a long, tulle tutu and with a silver princess's crown in her curly, long brown hair, spun around the restaurant as patrons and her parents looked approvingly on. We didn't know the occasion for her costume or her glee, perhaps it was her seventh birthday, but all of us were dazed as we watched her perfect limbs, her freedom of movement, her boldness unchecked and unhampered as we waited for our food.

On January 16, 2016, the *Bietigheimer Zeitung* reported that two witnesses, joggers on a dirt path in nearby Möglingen, had come forward to aid the "cold" case of the murder of Nadine Ertugrul. They informed police that they had often seen Nadine E. from 2014 to September 2015 between the hours of 5:00 and 8:00 p.m., the hours of their customary exercise, conversing with a "dark-skinned" fiftyish well-groomed man in a dark suit and sunglasses. Nadine E. arrived jogging on foot as he arrived in a VW Passat CC from the exit off the A-81, they said, next to his rear license plate a graphic of a "multicolored striped elephant," "the signet of a manufacturer of paints." They'd seen the photograph of Nadine E. wearing black jogging tights, black camisole, and a yellow tank top, and recognized her by her customary exercise attire. By February 17, the identity of the fiftyish man was still unknown, and police began to speculate that Nadine E.'s murder might have been "random," rather than a premeditated act perpetrated by an acquaintance. They thought their clues might grow if they offered a reward for information leading to the perpetrator's arrest.

Over time, the perpetrator of the crime against Nadine E. might be caught and tried, perhaps sentenced. In the few months after her murder, the imagined reasons for Nadine E.'s death shifted, and they might continue to shift, if anyone cares to think about them. The immediate implied blame of those who follow the edicts of fundamentalist Islam, assigning Nadine E.'s death as an honor killing, were deemed ludicrous, and suspicion of the perpetrator shifted to another dark-skinned man who may or may not be Turkish, and whose allegiances have not been discovered. Now, it seemed, Nadine E.'s murderer might have been a friend.

What will we remember about Nadine Ertugrul five years from now?

Nadine E.'s makeshift shrine will appear in images archived online. The red heart balloons that had been tied to the stipes of her cross were gone in a matter of months, likewise the sea of votive candles and bouquets. The small wooden cross that read "Nadine" and "*warum*" rotted. There is no thirty-five-ton Victory Column looming on the skyline of Ludwigsburg, or any town, with a gilded angel perched on top to proclaim lasting victory over humanity's vicious war against women.

What is it, then, that a simple, modest shrine for Nadine Ertugrul should mark? Nadine daughter? Nadine wife? Nadine mother? Nadine woman who could take care of herself? What kind of shrine should be erected so that the great-granddaughters of Nadine Ertugrul understand something about the significance of her life and death, something that preserves the dignity of the singular, unique Nadine, something that acknowledges the continuous assault against 1.33 billion women and girls? What symbol of the Divine should be engaged to link Nadine with heaven?

Where should the stumble stone for Nadine Ertugrul be installed? The curb next to the parking spot on Eduard Spranger Street where her locked car was found? In front of the apartment complex in Eglosheim where she lived with her family until the night she disappeared? On Reuteallee near the blackberry thicket where her body was dumped? Like the other stumble stones installed by Gunter Demnig, should this one bear information similar to the victims of Nazi crimes against humanity: Nadine's birth date, maiden and married surnames, date of death, cause of death. If future viewers know any history at all, are allowed to know any history at all, the dates of Nadine's birth and death would make it unlikely that she would be mistaken as a victim of Nazi aggression, but by then, will anyone know about that distinction?

In August 2016, Nadine Ertugrul's estranged husband, Ramazan, was arrested, and in September 2016 he was charged with manslaughter for the murder of Nadine E. Ramazan was secular, had lived in Germany since the age of seven, and had no deep roots in Turkey. During the testimony provided to the court during his trial in January 2017, reported by Christian Walf in the *Ludwigsburger Kreiszeitung*, a different portrait of Ramazan was painted. Rather than a calm, well-adjusted, happy-go-lucky and involved dad working through an amicable divorce, witnesses drew a portrait of a distraught and jealous husband in a custody battle with Nadine E., a husband with financial difficulties, physical injuries that made it difficult for him to work, and a drug problem. Though police divers in Monrepos

Lake never recovered clothing from Nadine E., a strand of Ramazan's hair was found in Nadine E.'s car. Right after Nadine E.'s death, Ramazan cleaned their apartment top to bottom, with uncharacteristic thoroughness and zeal, according to testimony. Fibers from bicycle gloves were found on Nadine E.'s thighs, though Ramazan denied the gloves belonged to him. He had said Nadine E. had gone to Lidl the night she was killed to buy a loaf of bread for their daughters' Monday morning breakfast, but it was Nadine E.'s habit to go with her mother to the neighborhood bakery on Monday mornings to buy fresh bread for her daughters. The night of Nadine E.'s murder, Ramazan made cell phone calls to three different women.

In *"Die schwierige Suche nach der Wahrheit"* ("The Difficult Search for the Truth"), Walf summarized the suppositions in Nadine Ertugrul's case based on forensic evidence. It's possible that Nadine E.'s murderer was familiar with the area and knew that the nearby ditch lined with brambles further down Reuteallee was secluded enough to hide her body. This information might be important given the location of the murder, time of death, and assumed time for the discard of her body. No one mentioned how Reuteallee transformed at night—its gloom and the hulking long-bed trucks parked along the curb menaced in their silent presence, the truck drivers pulled off the road there presumably for a few hours of sleep. In daylight, a constant stream of cars turns around at the roundabout; a steady flow of foot traffic moves up and down Reuteallee. On the weekend, walkers enter Favoritepark by the gate adjacent to the roundabout at the dead end of Reuteallee, and bicyclists take a shortcut down Reuteallee through Favoritepark or out along the paved paths into the fields outside of town. Who would think about night's menace in that bustling daytime spot, except for other women?

Even if no one could see Nadine E.'s body in the brambles, pedestrians and bicyclists along Reuteallee began to smell the odor of decay, hidden neither by daylight nor dark.

After six days of testimony in January 2017, the focus of the murder of Nadine E. locked on Ramazan, but on February 6, 2017, Ramazan Ertugrul was found dead in his cell in Stammheim, near Stuttgart, after fashioning a noose from his clothing and hanging himself. He had been placed on a suicide watch, unsuccessfully. He left several farewell notes proclaiming his innocence.

Jochen Faber speculated that some will see Ramazan Ertugrul's suicide as an admission of his guilt. The court and police investigators see "The Case of Nadine E.," as it was known, in this way. Ramazan's lawyers, Amely Schweizer and Wolfgang Pantzer, want Ramazan and his family to be free of manslaughter charges, even though Ramazan is dead.

A few weeks after Ramazan Ertugrul's suicide in February 2017, I queried Christian Walf about controversy regarding Ramazan's arrest, given that he had been a Turkish immigrant and Nadine E. was an ethnic German. I asked if German immigration rights groups had been advocating in Ramazan's behalf. He said there was no controversy in this regard. Ramazan had become a suspect because of his relationship with Nadine E., Walf said. Ramazan's posts on Facebook of himself and his new girlfriend aired four days after Nadine E. was murdered. Yet his post on Facebook threatening suicide three months prior, while Nadine E. was still alive, was explained as a gesture of anger and despair after Nadine E. posted a photograph of herself and her new boyfriend, also on Facebook. Ramazan Ertugrul's allegiances were erratic, evidence suggested. Regardless of Ramazan's country of origin, his decades navigating the contemporary European landscape of women and men, the hyper-rage men display when "their" women, "their" wives, "their" girlfriends reexamine allegiances and rights, positioned Ramazan among the legion of the world's men who act out an ancient role. His manliness, his claims, his entitlement to curtail Nadine E.'s freedom made him not a Turkish fundamentalist following an ancient code of honor, or a predacious, oversexed brown-skinned man, but a man locating, embracing, and acting out a common, deadly trope against a woman. For all Ramazan's years he believed himself to be in a relationship of equals, a contemporary German man in a relationship with a contemporary German woman adept at taking care, when it became clear that Nadine was going to continue her life without Ramazan in it, witnesses who knew the couple asserted that Ramazan reacted with violent, deadly force.

If Ramazan Ertugrul was falsely accused, Nadine Ertugrul's murderer is still at large. Perhaps there is a flaneur along Reuteallee who stalked Nadine E. and thought the ditch where he discarded her body among blackberry brambles the perfect spot to hide the evidence of his crime. So far, this unidentified man was right. Perhaps a truck driver had seen Nadine E. on other nights at Lidl and designed a plot to murder her, or perhaps a man was having a bad night and took out his spontaneous aggression on Nadine E. as she walked from Lidl toward her car.

Nadine E. was smothered. There were no signs of struggle on her body, later stories reported. Care was taken to remove Nadine E.'s jewelry, her clothing, splay her legs and slash her neck after she was dead—premeditated staging of the corpse to make the progression of her death seem a rape and murder. A knife was never found. Forensic evidence proved the staging of Nadine E.'s body to suggest sexual assault to be a fiction, buying time.

There are conclusions to be drawn, but they are incomplete. Can the individual Nadine stand in to represent every murdered person on the planet? Can the sound of a single hand striking a drum resonate like a locomotive trying to move through stone?

I am humbled by the children of the world's Nadines.

Risk Assessment

IN EARLY 2015, WHILE VISITING MY SON EZRA IN London, I weighed the pros and cons with him of flying to Lviv, from Lviv taking a bus to Ratne. I thought I needed closure, thought traveling to Ratne could provide it. Russian troops had invaded Ukraine and subsequently annexed the Crimean peninsula in March 2014, and though Ezra seemed game to make the trip, I was timid, reticent, thought the journey ultimately unwise. I chewed on my decision. We ceased talking about going to Ukraine, and at the end of January, I returned to the United States. Ezra shared recently that he'd thought again of traveling to Kyiv just before Russia's invasion of Ukraine in February 2022 because he has close friends in Kyiv and imagined a stop in Lviv and north to Ratne. For many nights after our most recent Kyiv discussion, I awoke from nightmares in which I cowered in a cold, blacked-out bomb shelter that was really a rendition of the closet in my childhood basement that stank of mildew, where the sump pump motor ran constantly.

The last night of these nightmares, Susha appeared wearing a dress the color of the sky in the Chagall windows in St. Stephan's

Church in Mainz. She exited the blue door of the row house where Lenin had lived in London near Russell Square. On the stoop, she linked arms with her niece, Loraynne, my stunning cousin, daughter of Susha's little sister, Clara, who throughout her life insisted she was born in New York, not Ratne.

In my dream Loraynne wore a strapless, white satin, floor-length evening gown embroidered with lotus flowers, long white evening gloves. Her eyes had the teary sheen of the Virgin Mary weeping in Renaissance paintings, though in my dream Loraynne wore a grin.

Susha's short-sleeved dress fell in an A-line drape just below her knees. Her brocade evening bag hung open like a child's mouth stuffed full of grapes, to reveal my older sister's prized blue-glass shooting marbles, also known as puries. Susha carried a cyanide capsule wrapped in a white hankie with an embroidered *S* in green, an empty fifty-gauge red shotgun shell, and a compact mirror. I watched them from across the street, breathless, afraid to greet my grandmother, afraid she wouldn't remember my name, afraid she'd take the cyanide and die a second time. When I finally crossed the street, Susha put both hands on my cheeks. Her eye sockets were empty, and when I looked again, she wore gag eyes, the kind that dangle off the face on springs.

In life, Susha wasn't funny. She wasn't wry or sarcastic or cynical, and her English wasn't good enough to pun. She rarely laughed and seldom smiled, because her dentures didn't fit her well. They hurt her gums, which were always sore. She tapped her foot in apparent pleasure when she listened to the radio, Lawrence Welk playing polkas on his accordion. Though Welk grew up in South Dakota, Welk's parents were ethnic Catholic Germans from Odesa, near Kherson, the town my grandfather Harry fled. They loved polka, too.

Susha died in 1972, and for many years after her death I prayed after I recited the Shema before bed that I would never forget the sound of her voice. I have forgotten it, though, the pitch, the lilt,

her Yiddish accent, even if it's possible to accurately label her a
midrange tenor, as I continue stubbornly to do. Her voice wasn't
high-pitched, but it wasn't deep or hoarse. When my mother and
my aunties gossiped at Susha's kitchen table, she listened, slapped
her opened hands on the metal surface, dragged her chair along
the floor as she pushed back from the table, and rose, the sough
of her garters and her support hose rubbing against her rayon slip.
My aunties' voices soared and chirped, then dove into the gut-
tural depths of Yiddish as Susha filled the sugar bowl with cubes,
poured coffee, spritzed seltzer into her glass, or lifted the iron lid
of the pie safe on the stove and banged it down, trying to align the
nipple in its groove to seal the lid. She put a sugar cube under her
lower lip like a wad of chew, dunked an *eier kichel* in her coffee,
and sometimes the silence after she delivered an observation was
so thick that we could hear coffee soaking into each kichel's floury
cells along with her swallowing the film of sugar-spittle that formed
around her gums. Rather than the pitch and tones of her voice, it's
the sound of her cracking eggs slowly, carefully, along the rim of an
old, off-white, chipped coffee cup I remember, as she checked for
blood spots before she used the eggs to prepare French toast for my
younger sister and me on Sunday mornings. Maybe what I remember best is the sound of her gargling without her teeth before she
went to bed.

Most elderly people's hands are rough and dry, and hers were
no exception. Her knuckles were always swollen, and her fingers
bent like a witch's, fingernails thick and short and fungal. She wasn't
fair, towheaded, or blue-eyed like my mother, not a redhead like
me, nor did she ever turn completely gray. The backs of her hands
had purple blood-blotches the hue and size of ripe Italian plums,
and even an accidental glance alongside a chair would form a bruise
the size of a dime underneath her knuckles. She liked to bathe fully
submerged in her claw-foot tub only in summer, so late in life she
smelled like the dish towel she draped over a bowl of rising challah

dough, and of denture powder, and the wax and dye in cheap lipstick, which she insisted she apply thickly, in little red dove wings on her upper lip, a clown smile on the bottom. The drawer of the sideboard I had emptied before she moved to a one-bedroom apartment on Holly Street had the same lipstick and denture powder odor from kissing Esta Plat's letters a hundred thousand times.

Susha wasn't a toucher or a roly-poly cuddler. I'd never seen her kiss the lips of anyone, and when my sisters, Sheila and Renée, and I dutifully approached her for our obligatory pecks on her proffered cheek, her skin was always cold. My mother inherited her mother's ice, and so how curious to think of Susha opening the sideboard bottom drawer to caress a bundle of letters, rub them against her cheek, kiss them lightly so as not to smudge with lipstick, sprinkle them with the tears my mother saw her shed. What would she have done when my mother came upon her crying over a bundle of letters from Ratne? Susha beat her rugs and moved her refrigerator to mop behind it, and her power was not limited to her arms alone. My mother was like her to the nth extreme, stronger, her embarrassment turned to outward rage, to screams, to blows. Why would my mother want to save the letters that had caused my grandmother, and her, such wretchedness, even if that wretchedness defined a crucial portion of their DNA?

Once you discover what you've been seeking, into what archive do you place it? Who will swear allegiance to the map of such a vanished life?

"Jaw," my grandmother began, *aw* as in the *o* in *oy*, *da* the *a* as with a schwa, Susha trying, and failing, to pronounce my English name. I can't remember what she called my sisters. Her Shema at night before she fell asleep was exhaled like the panting of a hunted fox, and though my cheeks were never wetted by her kisses, I can still recall, when my younger sister and I slept at her house, the sound of her ragged breath on her feather pillow. One Sunday morning

when she'd been awake before us for many hours, I heard a muffled thwack, thwack, thwack coming from her summer kitchen and
thought she had fallen and was pounding on the stoop for help.
The sound was her wielding a hammer, the steel head striking white
butcher paper, underneath the paper a not-quite-dead white fish
that had wriggled across the linoleum on her summer kitchen floor
before she ground it into the mash she'd use to make gefilte fish.

I tried to take my dream-grandmother's hand and lead her across the
busy London street, but her hand was a hot iron. When I dropped
it, her left hand turned to pincers, and her right, with long, exaggerated fingers like El Greco painted. When she opened her mouth to
speak, there was a dab of dyed red beeswax on her yellow tongue.
"There," she said, responding to a question I'd forgotten.
    The street became a sewer culvert, men pursuing as I crawled
through sewage, trying to escape their grasp. Susha was gone, her
voice calling as though I were in the spiral of a conch, "Jaw-da,
Jaw-da!" A man's hot hand wrapped around my ankle, squeezed
it, pierced it with a fishhook. My body disappeared, the culvert. I
stood at the base of a tall, smooth wall, a ticket window fifteen feet
above my head, a cellar opening at street level without doors or glass
in the windows. Around the periphery of the wall, rats tore at the
breast of a dead pigeon. A long, orderly line of people stood behind me. All their coats were frayed at the cuffs and hems. They
spit streams of sunflower hulls that tangled in my hair. I shouted to
the ticket clerk that I wanted a ticket to Lviv, and the clerk yelled
back that the train to Lviv took fifteen hours and the ticket would
cost nine hundred euros, but, she said, "The Lviv you're going to
isn't your Lviv. The Lviv you think you're going to is smoke. If you
want to go to Ratne," she said, "you'll have to walk from Lviv." She
handed me a hawk's wing, my ticket. It stank the way a decomposing hawk wing stinks, like mold on lemon pith. I sank up to my
neck in gravel.

Fellow Ratner Yisroel Chait returned to Ratne in 1945. His recounting in the Ratne Yizkor book is like a dream, but it is not a dream. He goes to the Prokhid Hills and lies beside the burial mound where nothing is growing. All around the mound, saplings have sprouted—grass, weeds, clumps of burdock, but in this spot, this wound where dirt is piled, nothing grows. His chest becomes so tight he can barely breathe. His skin seems to shrink around his bones. A big hand presses on his breastbone, but it is not the hand of God. He has forgotten how to breathe, or eat, or think. He is re-evaluating his humanity, but he is failing at the task. The only real thing to him is pain. He hears a sound; at first, he thought it was a bird. When he listens harder, his wife is speaking as though hanging from a limb in a nearby tree. He knows her voice, the lilt, her pitch. She tells him to go away and never to return.

History Lesson

I N THE YIDDISH THEATER PRODUCTION OF A RE-staged *Hamlet,* performed in Ratne in the 1930s, *Der Ye-shive Bokher oder der Yidisher Martirer* (*The Seminarian or the Jewish Martyr*), young women playing supporting roles, Hora-tio and his minions, carry on as sprites. With cotton beards, mus-taches, exaggerated side curls, too-large skull caps or wide-brimmed black hats, and long black coats over pants once forbidden any woman wear, the lithe and youthful cast affect mock-scholar dili-gence. In a photo from the Ratne Yizkor book that translates as my-opic goofiness, their characters' gazes mock in-grown lives spent in pursuit of the unknowable Divine.

The actor playing Avigdor, the Yiddish Hamlet, returns early in the afternoons from his Haskalah-kibbutznik practice near the vil-lage of Kamin'-Kashyrs'kyi, where he was learning to drive a tractor, a skill he'd need on the kibbutz he hoped would welcome him into the secular world of Palestine. He had practiced his lines while driv-ing the tractor along a dirt path, after which he went to the farm-er's hen house to gather eggs, whose shells were warm and smeared with shit and straw. The farmer had a barn roof repair for him that required courage and finesse, because the actor playing young Avigdor had never climbed a ladder, let alone wielded a hammer or lined his lips with nails.

The Yiddish *Hamlet*'s plot is recognizable, with a shtetl twist. Just returned to town after studying at the Great Yeshiva in Vilnius, Avigdor, in character now, had learned that his father died from a broken heart after witnessing what he had suspected for the past ten years, namely, that his wife had been cheating on him with his stepbrother, Todres. Avigdor rushes to the synagogue to seek his mother, who is standing underneath the decorated chuppah, about to be married to Todres. Distraught about finding his father dead and his mother about to remarry, Avigdor throws open the curtains in front of the Tabernacle and sees not the Torah but a vision of his dead father's head. Extreme agitation and pondering ensue, self-doubt, guilt, self-loathing projected by scratches to the face that tear his cotton beard.

A Purim festival is the setting for act 2, where Avigdor and Esther/Ophelia are about to sign their ketubah to solemnize their marriage vows. Before Avigdor signs the vows, he's handed a letter that had been written by his father, who explains his wife Dvoyre's/Gertrude's infidelity. As in *Hamlet*, Avigdor is cautioned by his father's ghost not to take revenge on his mother, "honor thy father and thy mother," the ghost howls as reminder, but rather, the ghost urges, "punish your stepuncle."

"*Tsu zeyn oder nisht tsu zeyn*" ("To be or not to be"), Avigdor laments, feeling trapped, all of his choices leading him to death.

After Todres realizes that his adultery has been discovered by Avigdor, Todres starts a rumor and an innkeeper informs on Avigdor, accusing him of being a socialist. The innkeeper has written out an accusation, which he leaves on one of the tables in the inn. A friend of Avigdor's finds the letter/accusation and pockets it before the Polish police arrive. Violence ensues, scuffling on stage. A supporter of Avigdor's is beaten by Todres's followers, because the supporter criticized the new rebbe, Todres, whose word, though corrupt, is law. Like in the old days, and the new.

Todres condemns the heretic Avigdor to death by stoning. Dvoyre tries to intercede on her son's behalf, but Todres threatens her, and to escape his beating, she jumps out the window, just as Avidgor appears stage left, bloodied by Todres's henchmen. Avigdor discovers his mother, mortally wounded. She slips her wedding ring off her finger, gives Avigdor his father's wedding ring as a blessing for Avigdor's marriage to Esther, and dies.

A year has passed when the last act begins, and Avigdor has escaped from incarceration in a mental institution. Avigdor's friends think he'll show up at his mother's gravesite, because the day of his escape is the one-year anniversary of his mother's death, when her gravestone will be unveiled. Beautiful Esther is on stage in a state of high anxiety after visiting Dvoyre's grave. She meets a friend of Avigdor's on the road, and he tells her that Avigdor is in town. She receives the news with deep confusion. Feeling both betrayal and joy, she dies.

In the last scene of the play, Avigdor laments beside his parents' grave as Esther's shrouded body appears, carried by her mourners. Avigdor tears his hair in grief and jumps into her grave pit, sings the Kaddish for Esther and his parents, says, "We will be united in death," and dies. The chorus sings "Blessed is the True Judge," a paraphrase of lines from the Kaddish, and the curtains close.

Der Yeshive Bokher was played as a farce, a burlesque of esoteric Yeshiva seminary students from a bygone era, and an exaggeration of the wicked corruption of the village rebbe represented by the character Todres. Boris Thomashefsky, the great American Yiddish theater icon, sang and acted the role of Avigdor in the United States, and YouTube archives a rendition of him singing the final Kaddish in the play. Farcical or not, the Kaddish always moved the house to tears.

Dear Susha,

Even with my eyes closed, I see you and Harry riding the streetcar along West Colfax to watch Avigdor, that kvetch. Harry's watch chain dangles from his pocket.

Remember Gittel Klein? She sat in the front row of Ratno's auditorium in a yellow dress too tight across her tuchus. Such yashtsherkes she spilled when Avigdor sang the Kaddish, you'd think she was at her mother's funeral. They used the gate of the old cemetery in Kowel as a prop, no less. I think that was wrong, but on the other hand, the gate was hanging by one hinge after the last pogrom.

The village players, my eynikl [granddaughter] among them, made the rebbes look like fools.

Were they fools, Susha?

Were we?

Someday they'll make a musical of us, and everyone will laugh.

Menus

T HE LAST WEEKS OF MY MOTHER'S LIFE WERE SPENT in a hospice facility on Jewel Road, close to the Babi Yar Memorial Park south and east of Denver. Near the hospice, I had seen a fourteen-foot-long rattlesnake stretched across the bike path I had been riding on, jarring my thoughts as I tried to clear my heart and mind to accept that my mother was going to die that day or the next. Watching the thick, old snake slither off down the bank of Cherry Creek did not calm me, and for several minutes I pedaled faster than I ever had, my feet tingling as though anticipating being bitten. A bicyclist approached along the path riding from the opposite direction, and I wanted to warn him about the snake, but when I drew closer, I saw that he wore ear buds and couldn't hear me.

I said nothing about the rattlesnake to my mother. I sat with her as she waited at the dining table for her dinner, along with the other five hospice occupants in residence. It was late afternoon, and while the residents waited for their dinner to be prepared, we all watched as one of the occupants was shaved by his daughter. Why she was shaving him at the table was not explored, nor judging from her

brisk, jerky, no-nonsense gestures did she seem to think that performing her father's grooming at the dinner table was any of our
business. She unfolded a white barber's cape and shook it out a few
times, fanning all the diners with hot, stale, dusty air. Satisfied with
the cape, she ran her fingers through her father's thin, steel-colored
hair and fastened the cape at her father's neck. "*Annnana,*" he said.

"Okey dokey, Dad," she replied. "Good idea! We'll sing 'America the Beautiful' when I'm done." She swished her fingers in the silver bowl of warm water on the table, then depressed the button on
a can of Nivea shaving cream. Lathered up, her father's face wore a
white mask below the dark circles underneath his eyes, suggesting a
raccoon, and another woman at the table pointed and attempted to
laugh at him, her dusty vocal chords stretched like old piano wire.
When the daughter picked up the razor, her father threw his head
back, his Adam's apple a small mountain in his neck.

"What's taking them so long to serve our dinner," my mother
said, impatient as usual, brushing at the imaginary crumbs on the
table.

The daughter took long, straight swipes down her father's lathered cheeks. After each stroke, she swished the razor head in the
small silver bowl of water. The foam broke up into little white
puffs outlined with whiskers. Her father didn't seem to mind the
shave; his eyes were closed. The daughter had tried before her father's shave to start a game of cards, but only two of the residents
could hold them, and one of those scattered all the cards and yelled,
"Fifty-two pick up!" The daughter had picked all the cards up off
the floor, tapped them into a neat rectangle again, and filled the
silver basin at the kitchen sink. I thought from her patience and
her ingratiating cheerfulness that she must have been a kindergarten teacher. She finished up and wiped the stray bits of lather from
her father's face with an edge of the cape. A drop of lather landed
on the saber of the Shriners lapel pin her father wore on his thin

plaid sport coat, and she whisked that away as she polished the silver pin with a corner of his barber's cape. Her father didn't respond when she asked him if he wanted cologne, but she splashed it on him anyway.

My mother lifted her twisted pointer finger to her mouth and pulled down her lower lip, jabbing her blunted nail into her gums, her most recent gesture of anxiety after a lifetime of off-key humming and sweeping across the surface of everything with her open palm to rid the world of dust. "Mom," I said, "they're cooking it right now."

"The howling," she said, of the singing that had ensued around the table. "It's making me crazy." I gently took her hands away from her ears and dabbed a napkin at the blood that had collected in the corner of her mouth from where she'd scratched her gums. Her brittle skin was covered with bruises, her blood vessels vanishing, and I watched as the spot I had touched on her hand darkened into a maroon circle the size of a golf ball. The woman shaving her father glanced quickly at my mother's hands covering her ears, then went back to singing, louder. I should have appreciated the woman's take-charge forced levity, but I didn't. In that moment, I was resenting it, but if levity had been left to me, we'd all have been sitting in silence chewing on our blistered lips, listening to the glob of Crisco melting in the frying pan in the hospice kitchen.

The aides were dancing to "Hey Jude" as they fumbled with the switch on the kitchen fan, frying a batch of prawns breaded with crushed cornflakes and eggs, and while the greasy shellfish drained, they attempted a duet. No one had an appetite except my mother, but the aides cheerfully soldiered through the meal and chased it with vanilla ice cream drowned in strawberry sauce.

That evening, I reviewed the afternoon with my younger sister, including a brief rant about what the aides had served our mother for dinner.

There was silence on the line until my sister cleared her throat. "They ate German chocolate cake for breakfast yesterday," she said. "Mom seemed pretty happy that they honored her requests. It was her birthday . . . you know."

"I couldn't get here yesterday," I said.

"I'm reporting," she said, "not judging."

My family and I always planned our trips to Denver for the beginning of August to celebrate my mother's birthday and my older sister's, also the time the apricots on our tree when we lived in Oregon were ripe. Some years, we brought my mother fresh apricots, and others, dried, the few years when I had enough time between harvest and our long, hot drive from Oregon to Colorado, apricot nectar and jam. I don't recall my mother ever saying that she liked apricots, and when I think about the big fruit bowl on the counter in the kitchen near the stove when I was growing up, the pile of washed summer fruit was green table grapes and cherries, one or two nectarines, watermelon and cantaloupe in the refrigerator always carved and cut into cubes. My mother didn't like the fuzz on apricots or peaches, and dried fruit stuck between her teeth.

And so it was August again, my mother's last. My sisters and I were not prepared for her death, though I think my mother was prepared. She knew if her heart didn't fail she'd likely die of complications from dementia, and she made a conscious choice, if one can choose such a thing, to die alert, aware, and still intelligent. After the fried prawns and the strawberry sundae, which she seemed to enjoy, I helped my mother back to her room and she fell asleep. The next morning, my younger sister got the call informing us that the soles of my mother's feet were turning blue, that her body was "shutting down," an aide reported. In her room, I held a paper cup with a few drops of apricot nectar to her lips. She blinked her eyelids and shook her head no. "Dollies," she said, "I love you. But I want a beef taco from Taco John's." Pointing to the corner of the window above her bed, she said, "*Pavutyna*," Ukrainian for "spider web."

Watergate summer I worked at a salmon cannery in southeastern Alaska to earn enough money to pay tuition for my last year of undergraduate school. Petersburg, Alaska, was my destination in my first attempt at living at a distance from my family, my room in the cannery's cookhouse no wider than my mattress on the floor. My general delivery post office address didn't deter my mother, daughter of a woman who, after all, wrote letters for almost forty years to the dark void of the Old Country. My mother continued my grandmother's legacy, picking up what would become a thirty-one-year letter writing campaign to me, and eventually to my sons, who knew my mother primarily through her letters, her blue-lined stationery folded neatly in thirds and always with two crisp one-dollar bills tucked inside, so that they could go to the corner store on C and Fourth Street in La Grande and treat themselves to a handful of penny candy.

My mother's grief was raw that Watergate summer of 1974. She still grieved for her mother and in the spring of 1974 my parents divorced. Being far away from home and home's troubles seemed like an ideal salve for me, though I was not as far away from home as Ratne. My mother's letters to me in Alaska did not mention my father, whom she pined for, or Susha, whom she grieved for, but rather the miraculous abundance of juicy raspberries in my older sister's backyard garden, her peonies and the pesky mint that grew along the garden's edges, the progress of the Denver Zephyrs, the weeks-long hot spell in July. I thought describing a kayak paddle across the Narrows to Kupreanof Island during a windstorm would terrify her and make her worry for my safety, likewise an aborted hike up Petersburg Mountain in torrential rain. I wanted to tell her how wretched it felt to watch an old Tlingit man crying in the bar in Petersburg over the death of the last elder from his family, without my being able to speak his native language, though she already knew what the death of culture feels like.

The next year, when Gerald Ford was president, I moved first to Berkeley to continue my study of Chinese, and then across the Pacific to Taiwan, to teach English. My mother's redacted letters arrived at my host family's home on Wuchun Lu in Taichung City on special blue-gray airmail stationery twice a week, like clockwork. Not only did Taiwanese censors redact her letters, she redacted her deepest fears, concerns about her health, the myriad family chores she foisted on herself, the tedious care involved in monitoring the painful, protracted deaths of all her siblings. Instead, she described the Fourth of July fireworks she watched from her front porch with my younger sister, my older sister's work with The Legal Aid Society, how handsome our cousins the Klein twins on Hudson Street had become, how she loved the scent of mowed grass and petrichor. I had never tried to share with her the texture of a day spent riding an old bike my host family loaned me along the high dikes outlining the rice paddies on the edge of Taichung City or to describe the shame I felt as I was chased down a dike's dirt road by an angry farm woman waving her fists at me, shouting to get my ugly, foreign, big-nosed mug away from her tender shoots of rice. I never wrote to say the taste of a deep-fried potato-and-onion pancake reminded me of Susha's potato kugel or to confide that *mugua niunai*, pureed papaya blended with ice and milk, was the only thing that stopped my stomach from aching. The night I had arrived in Taipei, there were fireworks and a street party outside of my hotel to celebrate the death of Mao Zedong, and the next night, a public execution of a common thief broadcast on TV. The first night in my host family's home, a thief tried to scale the high cinder block wall outside my bedroom window, which plunged me into a trauma loop that lasted for the duration of my trip.

Our letters to one another were always superficial. The kind-looking, relaxed woman on the mortuary gurney, with her hair so soft and freshly washed and combed, was a new aspect of my dead mother. In life she raged, and after graced us with her silent, thick disdain. Even dead, she was still the mother who had beaten me and my younger sister with a long wooden paddle.

But, really, on history's scales, what's one beating, or even several, compared to what humans in their hubris and their rages do to entire populations? Better to say that my mother wrote letters that I have saved, meticulously, and now, I have mine to her in shoeboxes in my closet.

I never asked my mother in a letter how a woman taking care moves about the world. The humid air in Taichung City smelled like crushed spiders, the creek near my host family's home like duck shit, not like the frangipani I described to her wafting on the breeze. It was in those first letters from Taiwan over several months that I began to see a distillation of my mother's life, her grief and depression hidden, our dissolving family whole in her imagination, the Holocaust a tribulation of some other tribe. Likewise, I hid my life from my mother, the woman I was becoming, the world I was encountering. To her I became the cowgirl rabba of La Grande, organizer of grand celebrations of the victory of the Maccabees or the Jews' exodus from Egypt. Really, I was mostly unsuccessful in rallying a handful of unruly Jews for potlucks in the Quaker Friends' Hall, where it seemed, no matter what, we always had chopped liver. My mother knew my pantry was full of vegetables I grew and preserved for winter like an industrious bubbie from the Pale, but I never spoke to her about the shelves of varenye I stockpiled, shoring up against the incipient anti-Semitism all around us.

Weronika

M Y SONS ASKED WHO MY DOPPELGÄNGER IS AND where she lives. I thought to say my doppelgänger is the past, but what I meant to say is that my doppelgänger was a woman who lived many years before I was born. I look for her in photos from the 1940s, but I have yet to find her. She is my Weronika.

In the late 1990s, my sons passed around a photo their friend had shared with them of a woman at a party in Argentina. They were excited by the photo and said the woman looked like me. The photo was taken by J—, the father of their friend, a man who left his family and reinvented himself as a river guide in South America. Now he owns a winery near Mendoza.

At first, I was nonplused that the father sent the picture to his daughter, as J— and I weren't friends, only the kind of casual acquaintances people are in small towns. Upon reflection, I was further mystified, then offended that the father had sent the photograph back home, because the woman was at least two decades older than I was then, looked like a bruja, I thought, a witch, same tribe as

me, half-crazed, tall, bony hands, wizened, probably drunk on one
of the amazing Malbecs famous in that region. She held a glass of
wine in one hand, an overgenerous pour, and with the other, a tiny
cracker. Her hair had the same wiry kinks and curls as mine, but it
was shorter. Though the photo was in black and white, it seemed
that she might have had red hair, or at least she wasn't gray. There
were several other people gathered around her in the photo, five or
six. Everyone seemed to be having a good time. I was upset because
I thought myself more attractive than this woman, yet the father of
my children's friend was so struck by the resemblance to me, I began
to wonder if, in fact, I don't see myself as others see me, if in fact, my
double could be walking around on the streets in Madrid or Berlin
or Prague or Washington, D.C., or the factory town of Ratne, and
I'd walk right by her, recognizing neither one of us.

Over time, I have grown less offended by this photograph;
mostly, the woman looked then as I do now, except I'm shrinking.
Recently, a student told me I look like a Celtic witch who performs
miracles. I assured her I don't perform miracles, but she didn't believe me.

As a point of fact, as I have said, many Jews from Volyn Province
emigrated to Buenos Aires in the 1920s and 1930s, including many
families from Ratne. One of those emigres to Buenos Aires had described the Ratne of her childhood as idyllic. Maybe that woman
knew Esta Plat. Maybe the woman drinking Malbec at a party in
Argentina had relatives from Ratne, cousins who were cousins of
Esta Plat.

Maybe one of my descendants a few decades from now will find
the photo of the woman from Argentina and flip it over to see if
someone had written names to identify the people in the photo. My
mother did this for me when I asked about the few photos we had
from the Old Country. Maybe one of my sons will have written, *J—
said this woman reminded him of my mother.*

EPILOGUE

Dear Susha,

   Here is the map to my bees. You will have to cross the swamp to find them. This is my secret hive. It belonged to my mother. She died before the current trouble. You remember the taste of her honey; the bees flew all over the country for us. Once, there were sunflowers throughout the land more numerous than stars.

   If you have lost me, find me with the bees.

ACKNOWLEDGMENTS

"Sad Angel" first appeared in *Rock and Sling: A Journal of Witness*. "Augury" first appeared in *Boulevard*, both in slightly different form.

In addition to the sources and materials I have woven throughout *Your Eyes Will Be My Window*, the works of several writers have been essential in the shaping of this book, for which I am deeply grateful: Joan Didion (everything), Timothy Snyder (*Bloodlands*), Yehuda Bauer (*The Death of the Shtetl*), Dan Porat (*The Boy: A Holocaust Story*), Svetlana Boym (*The Future of Nostalgia*), Rachel Eisendrath (*Gallery of Clouds*), Esther Kinsky (*River*), Jenny Erpenbeck (*Visitation*), Adam Zagajewski (*Two Cities: On Exile, History, and the Imagination*), Masha Gessen (*Words Will Break Cement*), Christa Wolf (*Accident*).

Historian Nicole Howard, thank you for the many conversations and insights that helped me conceptualize the tugs of oral history and archival data.

Special thanks to many gracious people who welcomed me in Germany and Israel, and who otherwise supported me in myriad ways while I was writing this book. In Germany, thank you to Peter

Dines, whose tireless work facilitated my residencies at the Ludwigsburg University of Education. Thank you to Loni Dines, Christoph and Heide Brudi, Jan Hollm, Hartmut and Margo Melenk, Judd and Kathy Koehn, Peter Fenn and Dani Arcularius. Jochen Faber and other members of the Stolpersteine Initiative Ludwigsburg, Walter Mugler, Andreas Nothardt, and Christian Rehmenklau, thank you for your dedication and willingness to meet with me; likewise thank you for the *Stolpersteine* tour of Stuttgart North, Jupp Klegraf. Thank you Harry Grenville, Rainer Mayer, Martin Hartmannsgruber, Stefan Kuhnle, Christian Walf, and Claudia Dulcius Bäder for sharing time and expertise with me.

In Israel, thank you Yochai Ben-Ghedalia, Josef Gelston, Claudine Schwartz-Rudel, and David Mevorah for meeting with me.

Many thanks to the librarians and archivists who assisted me at the United States Holocaust Memorial Museum Library in Washington, D.C., the Wiener Holocaust Library in London, the British Library in London, Yad Vashem in Jerusalem, and the Central Archive for the History of the Jewish People in Jerusalem.

Piotr Florczyk and Melissa Kwasny, thank you for your insightful reading and comments on my book.

Nicole Gratch, thank you for giving me the tools to write with clear-minded purpose during a pandemic.

Courtney Denney, Nicole Walker, Beth Snead, and Lea Johnson, thank you for the care you have given to my work.

Several stipends and sabbaticals provided by Eastern Oregon University made much of the travel for my research possible, for which I am grateful. Thank you to colleagues along the way who have listened to iterations of this book: Megan Kruse, James Crews, Christopher Howell, Lidia Yuknavitch, Justin Hocking, Carter Sickels, Jen Boyden, Ian Boyden, and to former students whose engagement with the elasticity of prose has enhanced my own: Robert Stubblefield, Aby Kaupang, Eden Kruger, Stacy Heiney Perrou, Maggie Byrd, Theresa Hamman, Stephen J. Jackson, Neil Hetrick,

Jamie Mueller Grove, Cheyenne Valade Maszk, Amy Parker, Althea Huestes Wolf, Gabriel Boehmer, Kirsten Johnson, and many others. Cheyenne Valade Maszk and Jamie Mueller Grove, thank you for writing with me on Sunday evenings.

For the love and support all the years I have searched for Esta Plat, thank you Joshua Axelrod, Ezra Axelrod, Tara Vanacore, and David Restrepo; your creative work and advocacy inspires and instructs me. David Axelrod, your steadfast allegiance to shaping life through poetry and prose bolsters me. Thank you hardly seems enough to express how crucial you have been on this journey, our journey.

This book is dedicated to my grandchildren, Silas and Vera Axelrod.

NOTES

I consulted several versions of the Ratne Yizkor book, one of many multiauthored volumes written after World War II by survivors of destroyed towns and villages throughout eastern Europe, including the *Memorial Book of Ratno; The Life and Destruction of a Jewish Town in Volin (Ratno, Ukraine): Translation of Yizker-bukh Ratne; dos lebn un umkum fun a Yidish shtetl in Volin*, trans. Gloria Berkenstat Freund, ed. Jacob Botoshansky and Itzhak Yanasowicz (Buenos Aires: Former Residents of Ratno in Argentina and the U.S., 1954) and *Ratno: Story of a Destroyed Jewish Community: Translation of Ratne: Sipura shel kehila yehudit she-hushmeda*, ed. Nachman Tamir (Tel Aviv: Former Residents of Ratno in Israel, 1983). As in many other towns, these anthologies of oral history and photographs were written in Hebrew, Yiddish, and translated into English.

The title "Your Eyes Will Be My Window" is a line from the poem "The Angel in the Forest" by Berlin poet Gertrud Kolmar, from her collection *Dark Soliloquy: The Selected Poems of Gertrud Kolmar*, trans. Henry A. Smith (New York: Seabury, 1975), 203–5. Kolmar's line is "Your eye will be my window." Kolmar's poems were originally collected in *Gertrud Kolmar: Das lyrische Werk* (München: Kösel-Verlag, 1960).

The reference to A. M. Klein is from his poem "Dialogue," from the collection *A. M. Klein: Selected Poems*, ed. Zailig Pollock, Seymour Mayne, and Usher Caplan (Toronto: University of Toronto Press, 1997), 29–30.

The title "Songs for a Blue Piano" is suggested by the poem "My Blue Piano" by Else Lasker-Schüler, in *My Blue Piano*, trans. Evan Boland (Portland, Ore.: Tavern Books, 2014), 17.

The gift of the pheasant narrated in "Feasts" was recounted, in part, during several conversations with Heide and Christoph Brudi. Its embellishment is mine.

The woman from Israel narrative in "Another Set for *Brundibár*" was recounted, in part, during a conversation with Rhonda Shafner. Its embellishment is mine.

The phrases from Friedrich Hölderlin's poem "Evening Fantasy" are translated by Maxine Chernoff and Paul Hoover in *Selected Poems of Friedrich Hölderlin* (Richmond, Calif.: Omnidawn, 2008), 87.

"Blue Moon" is my retelling of a traditional Yiddish folktale.

The title "The Pulse of Your Quietest Word" is a line from the poem "I'm Soaked through with You" by Rachel Korn, from the collection *An Anthology of Modern Yiddish Poetry*, selected and translated by Ruth Whitman (New York: October House, 1966), 34–35.

Yashtsherkes (tears) is from an idiomatic Yiddish expression, "*lakhn mit yashtsherkes*," literally, "to laugh with lizards," connotatively, "to laugh with tears," noted in a letter by David L. Gold and published in the *New York Times*, June 22, 1986.

Pavutyna, Ukrainian for "spider web," was recalled by Renée Varon.